HELPING YOUR DYSLEXIC CHILD

A Step-by-Step Program for Helping Your Child Improve Reading, Writing, Spelling, Comprehension, and Self-Esteem

Eileen M. Cronin, Ph.D.

Prima Publishing

Library of Congress Cataloging-in-Publication Data

Cronin, Eileen Marie.
Helping your dyslexic child: a step-by-step program for helping your child improve reading, writing, spelling, comprehension, and self-esteem / Eileen Cronin.
p. cm.
Includes index.
ISBN 1-5595-8290-1
ISBN 0-7615-1004-4
1. Dyslexic children—Education. 2. Dyslexic children—Education—Parent participation. 3. Language arts—Remedial teaching. I. Title.
LC4708.c76 1997
371.91'44—dc20 92-42948
CIP

97 98 99 00 01 AA 10 9 8 7 6 5 4 3 2 1
Printed in the United States of America

How to Order
Single copies may be ordered from Prima Publishing, P.O. Box 1260BK, Rocklin, CA 95677; telephone (916) 632-4400. Quantity discounts are also available. On your letterhead, include information concerning the intended use of the books and the number of books you wish to purchase.

Visit us online at http://www.primapublishing.com

To Mary Margaret
whose triumph over dyslexia
was the inspiration for this book.

Contents

Foreword

The foundation of remediation of reading problems is recognizing the individual as a unique person. Such recognition respects the child's insights, feelings, and distinctive ways of viewing the world and acting in it. As her one-time student and long-time colleague, I have watched Dr. Eileen Cronin apply this principle with great wisdom and sensitivity in her own practice.

Now I find her rich experience wonderfully crystallized in this book devoted to parents and educators of those termed "dyslexic." Some of the lessons I have learned from her and find affirmed in this book concern the importance of social communication and the joy to be found in serving people. Above all there is the lesson that everyone deserves an advocate whose caring is constant, although largely invisible, and whose vision influences what the person can become. Dyslexic people, like all people, can develop their potential by accepting their distinctive traits, uncovering hidden talents, and relishing the love, faith, and guidance of committed parents and teachers. Dr. Cronin is one such teacher, and this book is her act of love.

—Mary Delia Lanigan

Acknowledgments

Many thanks to all who helped me to write this book. Such an undertaking could not have come to completion without the many parents and children who contributed to this book with their questions, their need for help, and their belief in themselves. I thank all the dedicated teachers from both public and private schools who participated with me in seeking to become better equipped to help children and adults with learning problems.

To all the teachers at the Institute who inspired me daily by their commitment, expertise, and love for children and the learning-handicapped adult.

To my dear and long-time friend, Mimi Foord, who is gifted in many areas and from whom I learned so much about early childhood.

To Mary Margaret, who taught me more about dyslexia than I ever heard at any conference or read in any book.

To Mary Lanigan, my dear friend, for her interest in this book and the help she provided for me in so many ways.

I thank Duane Newcomb for his professional supervision in preparing this manuscript, and thanks to all my friends who urged me to write this book and kept asking, "When is your book coming out?" Well, here it is, my friends, and thank you for your support and encouragement.

About the Author

Eileen Cronin, Ph.D., has worked with learning disabilities for over thirty-five years. She has a doctor's degree in philosophy from the University of Fribourg in Switzerland. She has been a teacher and principal at the elementary level, a professor of education, a chairman of the education and special education departments, and the program director of the Ed.D. program in Leadership and Renewal at Lincoln University, San Francisco. She is the founder of the Ellen K. Raskob Learning Institute and was its director from 1960 to 1980. She is also the cofounder of the Robert P. Raskob Educational Leadership Services, Kentfield, California.

She has been a consultant to the Model School Program in the Richmond School District, Richmond, California, and a visiting professor in education at the University of California, Berkeley. She is a recipient of the Phoebe Apperson Hearst Distinguished Woman of the Year Award, for work with Mexican-American preschool children in language development, and a recipient of the distinguished service award from the Richmond School District. She has also written extensively on learning difficulties and reading improvement.

Introduction: Answering Parents' Questions

> A child helped today is a person fulfilled tomorrow.
>
> —*Eileen M. Cronin*

Most parents who are told by a teacher that their child has dyslexia are confused by the label: They do not quite know what it means. Is their child afflicted with some kind of mysterious handicap? They may also be told that their child cannot learn to read or cannot remember words nor recognize them when reading.

Parents may first wonder if the teacher really knows their child. Then they may ask themselves why the teacher can't do something about the problem. The child seems so bright at home. What went wrong? Are they to blame? Did they do enough? Did they do too much?

Of course parents aren't to blame; however, as Sally L. Smith, a nationally known expert on dyslexia, says in her book *No Easy Answers: The Learning Disabled Child at Home and at School,* there are things parents can do as soon as they discover their child is dyslexic to help him or her acquire the necessary skills for school success.

> Parents and teachers must become committed advocates for children, especially for those who have difficulty learning at home and at school. Parents and teachers must accept the premise that all children can learn and be successful in school—and in life. They must guard as a sacred and privileged responsibility the right of every child to grow, to mature, to work, and give them time to learn and practice those skills that help them become whole human beings.

With that in mind, I will answer some of the questions I hear most from parents.

Does my child have dyslexia?

It is extremely risky to use labels, particularly the label *dyslexia.* Historically, the term has meant different things to different people. To the clinical psychologist or neurologist, it means a condition reflective of "minimal brain damage" or "minimal brain dysfunction," a condition also called *word blindness.* To the educator, it implies a specific reading disability exhibited by a child with normal or above-normal intelligence and normal vision and hearing who receives the same instruction as other children.

However, simply because a child has not learned to read through conventional instructional methods does not generally mean that he cannot learn to read with instruction that is individually tailored to his particular learning style. This will be covered in detail in Chapters 1 and 7.

Parents are often held responsible for their child's behavior and urged to become better parents. Does this mean that I am to blame for my child's inability to read?

No. There is nothing in the research literature on dyslexia to indicate that it is caused by the parent-child relationship.

Parents' behavior is not responsible for dyslexia. In fact, in most cases, parents can do things to help their dyslexic child: They can build up their child's sense of self-worth and provide him with opportunities to overcome his reading weaknesses. It also helps if parents have a support group in which they can discuss the problems they are facing. When parents get together to talk about their children's problems, they are usually relieved to find that they are not alone.

A few months ago, I read an article that warned against teaching young children the alphabet. Do you recommend teaching the alphabet?

Yes. Children should be taught to recite the alphabet as soon as possible. The ideal time for a child to learn the alphabet song is when he is able to repeat rhymes of any kind. It is not yet necessary to have the child identify the letters in their cursive or printed forms or to have him associate letters with reading.

Through recitation, the child will acquire a knowledge of alphabetical sequence. His familiarity with the sounds of the letters will later give teachers a base on which to build visual and phonetic instruction.

The child could also be taught other things that have a natural order, such as the days of the week and the months of the year.

During a conference with a psychologist, I was told that my child had a specific learning problem. What should I tell my child about his learning disability?

Tell your child that even though he is bright and capable, he will need help with some school tasks. Reassure him that people have different strengths and weaknesses; for instance, some can't carry a tune, and others can't play golf or tennis.

Tell your child that he is fortunate that the problem has been discovered, and with help, he will learn to handle it. Reassure him that *he* is not the problem, rather that he has a skill problem and is a wonderful person regardless.

When my child fails to learn to read, is it always because he is dyslexic?

No. Not learning to read may indicate a number of other causes such as delayed readiness or lack of early developmental skills.

When should I have my child tested for dyslexia?
I caution parents about making a premature diagnosis. Brain cells mature at different rates and at different ages; it is not possible to differentiate between immaturity and a learning disability until the child begins school tasks (around first grade). Then you can see if your child tends to confuse letters, letter formation, and letter sequence. However, you should still not try to diagnose dyslexia at this point, because all young children tend to confuse letter formation when first introduced to letter symbols. Test for dyslexia if the child consistently mixes up letters and words even after a great deal of instruction.

What do you think about the use of mechanical devices, such as blurring scanners (a device that flips letter cards up and down quickly), in the early diagnosis of dyslexia?
I am skeptical of mechanical devices or any other contrived means of testing a young child because of the anxiety such tests cause him. There are few behavioral conditions that a parent cannot detect by observation; delayed maturation skills, faulty visual understanding, and hyperactivity are readily observed and easily alleviated through games or creative activity.

If my preschool child shows signs of hyperactivity, overaggression, or short attention span, should I seek professional help?
Yes, by all means. Start by bringing it to the attention of the child's pediatrician, and perhaps a pediatric neurologist, both of whom are well qualified to make a distinction between a neurological problem and a maturational lag. Early treatment for any physical difficulty may alleviate a problem before a child reaches school age.

Is there a critical time to begin treatment for dyslexia?
Yes, after the first year of school and after maturational deficiency has been ruled out. Observation of a persistent difficulty with letters and words over a period of three or four months indicates the need for therapy, and the sooner you start to correct the problem, the more effective you will be.

It is important to protect the child against repeated failure and discouragement.

Should I inform the teacher if I help my child at home or if I hire a tutor?
Yes. In general, teachers are willing to cooperate with parents to help a child who has difficulty learning. Parents should contact the teacher, ask about the child's progress, and arrange a meeting. It is advisable to create a school program specifically for the child, which is called an *individual educational program (IEP)*. The IEP is designed to set goals and develop teaching techniques that benefit the child. (See Appendix F for the rights related to an IEP.)

When will I know that my child is ready to discontinue special instruction?
When test results for reading skills measure one full grade above actual grade placement, you can assume that your child will be able to operate comfortably and independently at grade level.

Some dyslexic children, however, may require special help for as long as they have learning difficulties, and they may have these difficulties for years. Dyslexics have problems not only with academics but also with organizational and interpersonal relationships. A dyslexic child is very likely to require continued psychological support and encouragement through adolescence and into adulthood.

Is there really hope for my dyslexic child?
Definitely. This is a problem that can be solved by pulling together as a family to give the child special help at home and at school. With proper support, dyslexic children become adults who are capable of performing brilliantly in such nonverbal fields as auto mechanics, architecture, and engineering, as well as in more traditionally artistic pursuits. Many distinguished achievers were dyslexic: Edison, Rockefeller, Einstein, Rodin, Michelangelo, leaders in business, industry, sports (Nolan Ryan), and entertainment (Cher), and even respected writers. My best advice is to live

in the present; the future will take care of itself if you deal with the present realistically. Many men and women who suffer from dyslexia lead successful lives.

Is dyslexia inherited?

One parent asked me if dyslexia was an illness that could be "caught." It is in no way contagious, but evidence does seem to indicate that dyslexia is passed from parent to child. In Sweden in 1950, Bertil Hallgren's research on twins established that dyslexia is transmitted genetically. By tracing family histories, he showed that dyslexia is a sex-linked dominant trait that manifests itself in generation after generation. Most studies of dyslexia report that boys are affected far more frequently than girls. This unequal distribution is also found in the higher incidence of speech defects in boys.

I once asked a high school student with a tendency toward unusual spelling if anyone in his family had a similar problem. "Oh, yes," said the boy. "You should see my father's spelling. He's worse than I am." In speaking with many families after testing, I often hear fathers say they experienced the same problem going through school.

Is an intelligence test an accurate reflection of a dyslexic's abilities?

Dyslexics fall into the same intelligence curve as the rest of the population: Some are average; some are bright or even gifted; some are below average.

Intelligence tests, however, must be interpreted with caution. The results of IQ tests taken by dyslexics indicate only how they functioned at the time of testing, and the results are called "functioning scores." Of course the dyslexic who cannot read, write, or spell cannot be expected to test well. This means that a test given to a child or adult who is dyslexic may not be valid. Retests often show that, after special instruction adapted to the dyslexic's specific problems and style of learning, improvement occurs—even on standard IQ tests.

When is my child ready to start school?

The school assumes that when your child is approximately six years old, he is ready for school tasks. But some children simply may not be ready, especially if they are immature, dyslexic, or lack early skills. Every child has his own time schedule for intellectual development.

Only you can determine, through your observation, if your child is ready to enter school. Only you see your child every day and only you can tell when he has mastered the early skills. Both parents and teachers should remember that, at age six, a dyslexic may not be ready to translate his world of experience into the symbolic language of school tasks. Remember that you are dealing with a child who, for a long time, will need reinforcement by basic concrete manipulation—he will need to have connections made between learning and his own experiences. A dyslexic child takes longer to acquire skills for learning, and regardless of how well he may develop these, he will always have difficulty applying them.

Is my child immature or dyslexic?

Teachers and parents are often puzzled by the child who lags behind others when he begins to learn how to read. Is he immature or dyslexic? Both immature and dyslexic children have the same difficulties in the beginning reading stages, and all primary-grade teachers have both in their classes.

When a very young child is slow to achieve early childhood skills, it is difficult to determine whether he is dyslexic or not. The early periods of development are much the same for all children, and one child may appear to be a little slower than another because of immaturity. Remember, the brain develops in spurts. I encourage parents not to be overly anxious, to be mindful of the importance of early skills, to provide practice for them at every opportunity, and to watch for those marvelous spurts. Some children's difficulties come to an end with maturation, but the dyslexic never really quite overcomes his problems.

In the following chapters, I will discuss in more depth these and other questions you may have as the parents of a dyslexic child. There is much that you can do to help your child acquire needed skills. With your assistance, your child can learn to cope with most of the difficulties caused by dyslexia. He can learn to read, spell, and write and go on to live a full and very productive life.

Author's Note

Because an overwhelming majority of the children affected by dyslexia are boys (some 90 percent), I use the male pronoun almost exclusively. Readers should in no way construe this as being anything other than a reflection of this simple fact.

1

Is Dyslexia Real?

> The dyslexic's differences are personal, the diagnosis is clinical, the treatment is educational, the understanding scientific.
>
> —*Margaret B. Rawson*

As I have learned from my teaching experience, dyslexia is very real. It is so real that, by conservative estimates, it affects about 10 to 25 percent of children and an unknown number of adults.

Dyslexia, of course, encompasses more than slow reading or poor reading skills. It is a specific handicap that has plagued certain people, from childhood into adulthood, ever since language took written form. As a working definition, dyslexia can be considered a dysfunction of the part of the brain that processes nonlinear information. A dyslexic can be defined as a person who has a defective capacity for acquiring—in a "normal" amount of time—proficiency in reading, writing, spelling, and math.

When I first started to teach, I had a young boy who tried hard but who could never keep up with the others. When I asked him to read aloud, he kept mixing up the words. It took several months of working together before I realized he was dyslexic. Since that time, I have been able to help many of these children, and I now want to show both teachers and parents how to do the same thing.

In my classes and through my own research, I discovered that the dyslexic has many problems, both academic and nonacademic. Academically, the dyslexic has difficulty associating sounds with graphic symbols (letters and words) and extreme difficulty mastering the sequence of both written and spoken language. When the dyslexic attempts to piece together bits of information, the ideas themselves get lost in transit.

This shows up first in the inability to read well, spell correctly, and do math problems. The child cannot tell the difference between letters or words of similar shape. The letter *b* often gets mixed up with *d, p* with *q, m* with *n,* and so on. Some words get read backward (*was* becomes *saw*) or letters in the words get confused (*horse* becomes *house; now* becomes *new*). Dyslexics have long lists of so-called problem words such as these. Some children even write or print their names backward.

Letters and words can also become confused in speech; for instance, when a dyslexic child attempts to say *glass* or *cup,* he may start to say things like, "Oh, you know what I mean, the thing you drink with."

Spelling becomes particularly difficult. Words seem to be only jumbles of letters. The dyslexic will add, mix up, or drop letters, because he cannot picture in his mind what the word "looks" like. He may spell a word correctly when asked to spell it aloud but then write it incorrectly, unaware of the mistake.

Dyslexic children also never seem able to follow along when the class is reading aloud. Unfortunately, teachers often stop calling on these children because it is too time-consuming to listen to them stumble over words, mispronounce them, or get them mixed up in a meaningless jumble.

Nonacademically, dyslexia affects the ability to comprehend anything requiring linear thought—TV news, recipes, shopping lists, banking information, and many other tasks pertinent to daily living. Dyslexics can have difficulty understanding and carrying out directions; for example, if asked to go to the kitchen for some sugar, the dyslexic may forget what to bring back or may even forget to come back at all. A dyslexic taxi driver I met in Denmark when I was there studying dyslexia had a red band on his right wrist and a blue band on his left so he could remember how to make left and right turns.

Unfortunately, the effects of dyslexia extend beyond the classroom. If classmates taunt the dyslexic about his mistakes, the child's self-worth takes a tumble. The dyslexic may begin to describe himself as "stupid" or "dumb." To compensate for their discomfort, dyslexic children often become class clowns. This attempt to win recognition is usually overriden by the teacher's displeasure.

Conversely, the distressed dyslexic may succumb to his feelings of inadequacy by withdrawing into a shell for protection. I once worked with a fifth-grade boy who had been labeled a loner. He spent recess and lunch period alone and carried a book as a security blanket. He couldn't read it, of course. (I still believe he was making a statement about his desire to be able to read.)

Sometimes these children feign stomachaches or other ailments to avoid going to school. They don't talk about school and seem to lose that wonderful sense of curiosity most children possess. School becomes a bore. I have had many children in my classes who used all types of subterfuge to keep everyone, including the teacher, from knowing that they had a learning problem. One woman explained how her dyslexia had made her dread school.

"When I was in first grade I couldn't tell one school bus from another. They all looked the same to me. One day I was particularly puzzled, but one of my sister's friends told me to go home with her, and I did.

"When I got to the friend's house, her mother couldn't figure out what to do. I couldn't remember my last name, but I thought it was Green. In desperation, the mother called every Green in the phone book. Eventually, she found my grandparents and took me to them. But I was never able to explain to my parents that I couldn't identify the number of the bus."

As a student, this woman constantly felt harassed. She was embarrassed to do math at the board because it never came out right; she couldn't count money or tell time. She said, "My cousin finally taught me to remember which hand on the clock stands still and which hand moves around, but even now, at twenty-seven, it takes me a while to figure out what time it is."

She also had difficulty knowing right from left. Once when she was eight years old, her father let her run the lawn mower. He told her to go left, but she got confused and went straight, smashing the mower into a garbage can.

"In junior high school," she said, "I would tell my teacher I was ill, because I couldn't face reading and spelling. In high school, I would get lost trying to find my classroom because I couldn't remember whether it was on the first, second, or third floor."

Although this may seem like an extreme case, it's typical of the problems faced by many dyslexics. To make it more complicated, parents and teachers often simply don't realize what's wrong.

The History of Dyslexia

Dyslexia was first recognized in 1896 by a British school physician, James Kerr. He noticed that although certain children had good vision they could not read words. This affliction came to be known as *word blindness* and is still called that in England and in the Scandinavian countries.

Later, a German professor, Karl Kussman, labeled the problem *dyslexia.* This word comes from the Greek root *dys* meaning "difficulty with" and *lexis* meaning "word" or "language." However, dyslexia is so baffling that experts still struggle to find the right name for it, and educators search for better ways to help dyslexics survive in a world dependent on the understanding and use of language.

Initially, few educators attempted to help the dyslexic. Then in the mid-1920s, Dr. Samuel T. Orton, a neuropathologist and psychiatrist, became challenged by a sixteen-year-old who scored in the superior adult range on nonverbal tests but could not read. Dr. Orton devised a three-pathway approach using visual, auditory, and kinesthetic-tactile skills for helping dyslexics master language problems. Through this approach, dyslexics see the words, pronounce them, and become aware of the muscle movements of speech patterns. Later, at New York's Columbia-Presbyterian Hospital, Dr. Orton, in collaboration with psychologist Anna Gillingham and teacher Bessie Stillman, formalized the Orton-Gillingham approach so that teachers without medical or neurological background could easily understand and use it. This method is still employed today, especially by the Orton Dyslexia Society.

The Adult Dyslexic

There is no way to count accurately the number of adult dyslexics. The National Commission on Literacy reports that thirty million adult Americans, many of whom may be dyslexic, cannot read a classified ad, a newspaper, an insurance policy, their child's report card, or a note from their child's teacher. Many can't read instructions, follow recipes, or comprehend the full meaning of television or radio presentations, and their feelings of inadequacy often cause poor relationships both within the family and with colleagues at work. Dyslexics often respond inappropriately to social situations and, as a consequence, are misunderstood and often avoided. As one young dyslexic woman said, "I feel like a misfit. I always seem to say the wrong thing. And I can't remember small talk. I feel isolated. I have no friends. I'm a misfit and a loner."

Sometimes, an adult dyslexic can do his job well but still be penalized for being dyslexic. For instance, after struggling through college, one adult dyslexic went into printing and became a photolithographer. "I took up color separation and plate making, stripping, and other things that didn't require reading," he said. "I had to read to get the technical knowledge required to do the job, but I avoided jobs that would require other types of reading. Eventually, I became a department head."

After a few years, he became a publishing coordinator, which demanded that he know the quality of the work provided by different printers and that he serve as the liaison between authors and editors. This job also did not require reading and writing skills. "I would just communicate with both sides, and if there were any problems, I would get the people together and help them arrive at a solution," he said.

Finally, he was assigned to a microresearch program and developed a process that revolutionized the system. But a coworker was asked to do the technical writing.

"When we finished," he said, "I was called into the manager's office and told I had done an excellent job and would get a night out on the town. However, my coworker got a promotion and was sent to the national convention to present the paper that he wouldn't have been able to write without my technical knowledge. My manager told me that even though I had done 90 percent of the work, it was the other fellow's job to do the presentation and that was more important. I was discouraged. My inability to read and write was causing me a lot of problems. Another time, a manager asked me to write my information on the board for him and my mind went blank. I couldn't write a word."

It wasn't until then that he discovered he was dyslexic and began a remedial program. Now he is back in college and has a 3.6 grade point average.

As this example shows, many adult dyslexics working today were never identified during their school days. They still carry the scars of being called lazy, stupid, lacking in motivation, antisocial, or strange. They often cannot attain recognizable abilities and are haunted by past school failures. They frequently worry that their past failures will be revealed.

Many communities now offer remedial programs and support groups for adults in which members can share their ambitions and frustrations. In addition, dyslexics are aided by the availability of computer spelling and editing programs, which make writing or assembling reports much easier for them.

Identifying Dyslexia

Someone once said that "reading is talk wrote down." Words—the symbols of language—are an essential part of language skills, and their use (as well as the use of other symbols) is the dyslexic's problem.

The little boy who said "I can think okay, but I can't remember the words. I forget them. I can't manage them" was probably admitting his dyslexia.

Dyslexia is a complex language disability that—because it is related to memory and social problems as well as academic difficulties—is hard to isolate from other learning disorders. Expert researchers and teachers still struggle to understand what dyslexia really is and what causes it. Often, this dysfunction is identified only when a child begins school and is expected to acquire reading, writing, and spelling skills. (A clue that helps to diagnose dyslexia is bizarre spelling.)

All teachers, especially beginning teachers, have difficulty differentiating the dyslexic child from those who are immature, those with poor mental abilities, those with emotional difficulties, or those burdened with a congenital handicap. Even today, many teachers simply don't realize that a child who is having trouble with language is dyslexic; frequently, a teacher resorts to describing the child's external behavior. Many teachers have told a child's parents that he lacked motivation, was lazy, daydreamed, or was disruptive. None of these words accurately describes the problem.

Every child can learn if his abilities are identified and his learning difficulties are addressed.

Procedures for Identifying Dyslexia

When testing for dyslexia, trained clinicians generally rely on a reading and spelling test, the child's history, the family's history, and the results of a standard achievement test.

The procedure that many clinics and learning programs use to diagnose dyslexia is outlined below. At the end of the chapter, there is a test you can give your child to see whether he needs further examination.

Step one. Ask your child questions about his school life. For example, you might ask the following: Do you think you have a problem? What do you remember about learning to read and spell? What special help did you get from your teacher? Why do you think you couldn't learn to read well right away? How do you get along with your teacher? How do you get along with the other children? What subject do you like best? What subject is easy for you? Which one is hard? Do you need help now?

Children who are good students and who have few difficulties in school will answer these questions straightforwardly. The dyslexic, on the other hand, to protect himself from being thought stupid, often will devise a rather elaborate explanation for the difficulties or failures. Here are a few answers of dyslexics from actual tests. Answers like these are clues that, when considered with the other four steps, may indicate that a child is dyslexic: My first grade teacher was old and had forgotten how to teach. I petted a dog on the way to school and couldn't get my mind off of it long enough to learn anything. My teacher didn't like me and would never call on me. I was sick for a month and missed all the important stuff. I needed glasses and couldn't see the board but the doctor wouldn't give them to me.

Step two. Investigate the family history. Did mother, father, brothers, sisters, aunts, uncles, grandmothers, or grandfathers have difficulty with reading or spelling? Sometimes you will find that the child's brothers and sisters are having unusual problems with schoolwork, or that the father or mother had trouble learning to read or is still having difficulty reading. Often, the family members of true dyslexics have similar problems.

Step three. Evaluate the child's intelligence. Parents have a general idea of whether their child is smart, average, or a little behind. Whether you are a parent or teacher, when you evaluate a child, it is important that you do your own informal intelligence evaluation based on the child's conversation, interests, behavior, and history. Even if, as a teacher, you have access to a dyslexic child's IQ test, too often it will not accurately reflect his IQ, because it relies primarily on reading and writing to obtain results. In addition, dyslexic children learn to fear tests and therefore do not perform well. Fortunately, with remedial help, a dyslexic's score on IQ tests can be improved dramatically.

Step four. Give an oral reading test. Most teachers will know about and have available the Gray Oral Reading Paragraphs Test, though parents can sometimes purchase it in stores that specialize in learning materials. The test consists of a series of paragraphs, classified by grade level (first through twelfth grade), that judges the rate of the reading, the quality of the reading, and the reading recall. Below is an example from an actual test.

> Once there was a little pig.
> He lived with his mother in a pen.
> One day he saw his four feet.
> "Mother," he said, "what can I do with my feet."
> His mother said, "You can run with them."
> So the little pig ran round and round the pen.

Here is the same paragraph as read and rewritten by a nineteen-year-old dyslexic.

> There were a little goat.
> He lived with his mother in a pen.
> One day he was his front feet.

"Mother," he said, when could I do with my foot."
His mother said, "You could run with them."
So the little pig run rund and rund the pig.

If you can't get a copy of the reading tests, you can give the child an informal test using material at his grade level. If the child misses one out of ten words or ten out of one hundred words, the material is too difficult. Continue the test using lower grade levels until you find material the child can read without making any mistakes. That is his reading level, regardless of his grade in school. (To compute a child's expected grade level, subtract five from his age.)

Step five. Evaluate the child's spelling and writing. First, ask the child to spell words from a short standardized list that designates an intended grade level. Below are the words from an eighth-grade-level spelling list.

catch	clothing	suit	fell	walk
black	began	track	fight	grant
warm	able	watch	buy	soap
unless	gone	dash	stop	news

Here is how one thirteen-year-old dyslexic spelled them.

cach	clorthing	sut	fell	wock
black	began	track	fite	grant
worm	abl	woch	biy	sope
anless	gon	dash	stop	nus

Dyslexics generally make the following error patterns when spelling:

1. Reversals and inversions of letters (*d/b, q/p, u/n, t/f*) and of sequences of letters (*was/saw, felt/left, on/no, plea/peal, blind/build*)
2. Confusion of letters (*f/l, k/h, m/n*) and of small words (*of/off, at/it, of/if, me/we*)
3. Omissions of letters and syllables (*stad/stand, afaid/afraid, perstent/persistent, stike/strike, transportion/transportation, place/palace*)

4. Substitutions (*a/ the, off/ on, pretty/ beautiful, house/ home, woods/ trees, grand/ great*)

In the spelling example above, the child spelled seven words correctly and made substitutions or omissions in the rest—a good indication that the child is dyslexic.

Next, ask the child to write a short paragraph on any subject, such as his favorite person or his pet. Here is what one child meant to write.

> The dogs are getting bigger and their eyes are open well and in two weeks they will be walking real good and they are learning to walk now and they will be old enough to hold.

Here is what he actually wrote. Again, there are reversals, confusions, and omissions.

> The dog rae geting biger and their eis are open well, an in 2 weks thay will ben walking rel gool and they rae lneing to walk now and they will be old enof to hold.

These last two steps, when combined with the information from other steps, will indicate fairly accurately whether or not a child is dyslexic.

If possible, children should be screened as described above either before they enter kindergarten or before first grade. Older students should be evaluated before advancing to a higher grade. Parents and teachers should always ask for a complete examination whenever they suspect a child is dyslexic. Unless the dyslexic child is identified early and taught in a structured and consistent manner that suits his style of nonlinear thinking, he cannot learn to read.

The Parents' Dilemma

Parents are often confused by and unable to understand their child's inability to read. How could their child, who seemed perfectly normal and intelligent at home during the early years, be incapable of handling the learning tasks demanded of him at school?

Some parents may even overcompensate by trying to teach their child to read before he starts schooling. I don't recommend this. Reading is a complicated skill that depends on various areas of the brain that control the language function. There are many other activities that you can use to introduce your child to the symbols used for reading, math, and writing. These will be covered in detail in the following chapters. First, however, you should determine your child's level of ability.

Testing Your Child Yourself

If you feel your child may be having trouble in school, I suggest that you conduct the following simple test at home. The test is divided into two parts: school performance and a home observation test. The questions you should ask are outlined below.

School Performance

Ask your child's teacher the following questions: Does my child have friends at school? How does he get along with the other children? Is he included in playground games? Does my child follow directions and instruction in the classroom? Does he seem to have any physical problems, like not being able to hear lessons or see the board? Can he print or write? Paste? Cut? Draw? Does he mix up letters or words? Does he seem slow or inattentive with academic tasks?

The answers to these questions will provide some background information to complement the information you gather from the following observational test.

The At-Home Observational Test

Answer these questions from memory or while you observe your child at home. The individual questions may sound simple, but when all the information is put together, you will have a sense of how ready your child is for kindergarten or first grade (four to six years of age). Place a Y for yes or an N for no after each question or in the spaces indicated.

Motor skills

1. With a pair of scissors, can my child cut well (for his age) a circle ___, a square ___, a rectangle ___, a triangle ___?
2. Can my child run ___, skip ___, jump ___?

Motor coordination

3. Can my child color within the lines of a circle ___, a square ___, a rectangle ___, a triangle ___ in a way that seems appropriate for his age?
4. Can my child color within the lines of a picture in his coloring book?
5. Can my child walk a straight line, putting one foot in front of the other?
6. Can my child throw a ball?

Sense of space

7. Is my child certain of his right or left hand?
8. Does my child get confused about directions in space or time—right and left ___, up and down ___, behind ___, in front of ___, yesterday ___, tomorrow ___, days ___, months ___?
9. Can my child complete a six- to twelve-piece puzzle?

Memory sequence

10. Can my child follow a simple direction of two parts; for instance, "Pick up your jacket and hang it in the closet"?
11. Can my child remember three items and bring them to me; for instance, "Bring me your pencil, paper, and book"?

Language

12. Is my child's speaking vocabulary fairly good for his age?
13. Does he act out his ideas rather than use words?

Making choices

14. Can my child make independent choices; for instance, clothes ___, toys ___?

Social maturity

15. Is my child social with others ___, his brothers and sisters ___, friends outside the home ___?

Behavior

16. Does my child become frustrated when he can't do something—tie his shoes ___, find his clothes ___, have something he wants like food, candy, a toy ___?

If you answer no to five of the questions above, your child may have a problem with development. If after administering these two tests, you suspect that your child is dyslexic, then I suggest you request further testing from your school district or from a private clinic. If your child is diagnosed as dyslexic, you need to have him begin some type of remedial treatment at once. Help for school-age children can be found within some school systems. In such programs, the children usually work in small groups and receive special help daily during the reading, spelling, or language periods. If help in the school itself is not available, you could try private agencies, tutors, or college or university programs, which usually offer more intensive training.

While these programs can be invaluable, I firmly believe that you and your child's teacher can make a tremendous difference in his progress on your own. And that's what this book is all about. Dyslexia is not something that starts when the child reaches school age. A child begins to develop his motor and sensory skills at birth. Language skills usually develop organically, as the child hears conversations, is spoken to, is asked questions, or asks questions himself.

In the remaining chapters, I present a comprehensive and holistic program that any parent or teacher can easily use. I developed it during my many years of teaching and counseling; it has successfully helped dyslexic children and adults improve their reading, writing, and spelling skills as well as their social relationships, enabling them to lead more fulfilling lives.

2

The Growing Mind

Success in life comes one step at a time.

—*Eileen M. Cronin*

During the early years, parents often wonder whether their children will do well in school. Will they learn to read and write? Will they understand the teacher's instructions, follow directions, get along with the other children, and make friends? And finally, will they get "good" grades?

This chapter will discuss how children's minds grow, to help you better understand the dyslexic child's problems and to offer you some additional exercises you can use to help your child develop.

When your child goes to school, *learning how to learn* will be his most important lesson. Learning means more than receiving information and then responding appropriately to questions in order to get good grades or please the teacher or parents. Learning happens when someone becomes curious about something seen, heard, felt, or experienced and makes behavior changes as a result. The purpose of learning is to help your child adjust at home, at school, and in the world.

Because you are your child's first teacher, his success in school depends on early development in the home. I advise you not to push your dyslexic child but to become aware of his need to develop early skills as a foundation for solid early learning. You can do things at home to reinforce basic early skills—by setting up routines for dressing, eating, participating in family sessions, and playing alone or with friends. Such routines help greatly to prepare your child to respond to school tasks as other children do.

A number of school systems now give *readiness tests* to children who are beginning kindergarten or first grade. You can use these tests to gather objective information about your child's readiness for school and pinpoint those skills that might give him difficulty.

The dyslexic is betrayed in many ways by his lack of organization. Although he may be intelligent, he never seems to be at his age level academically. It almost seems as if he lacks the filing system in his brain that allows information to be absorbed, stored, and retrieved quickly and accurately. If these children fall further and further behind the expectations of each grade, they lose self-esteem and self-respect and are overcome by a sense of failure. This scenario is, of course, unnecessary.

You and your child's teacher must remember that a dyslexic is developmentally younger by three or four years than the other children in his classroom. And if it is discovered that the child cannot do the tasks required either at home or in school, expectations have to be lowered while you invent ways to help him establish a routine that meets his abilities.

The Development of Learning

Learning begins with the primitive physical responses of the infant and develops gradually into a lifelong adventure. How well your child learns to do school tasks depends on how well he develops early childhood skills during the first years of life.

Jean Piaget, the Swiss philosopher and psychologist, claimed that a child's mind develops in biological stages that follow a specific sequence. Although the stages are the same for all children, the rate of development from stage to stage varies with the individual. Every child is unique and special. When working with parents and teachers, I remind them that individual children develop according to their own growth patterns and time tables.

Levels of Development

Your baby will gradually develop from a reflexive, self-centered, and disorganized being into an organized, responsive child. During this development, your child's senses of hearing, sight, touch, taste, and smell become integrated into what is called *sensory intelligence.* He is able to recognize his parents' voices and associate them with food, playtime, and laughter. Later as the child crawls around on the floor, he inspects objects that catch his fancy because of their color and size and because he can grasp them.

This preschool stage is the bridge from the automatic physical reactions of the infant and early childhood skills to the demands of "real" school. The preschooler becomes more intellectually sophisticated and capable of "mental pictures" originating from motor activity and experiences. He begins to operate mentally on basic concrete information taken in from the environment, which is crucial to intellectual development.

For example, three-year-old Betty observed her brothers and sisters doing homework with their parents after dinner. One evening, she joined them, opened a book, and pretended to read. Her older sister saw her and called out, "Look, Mama. Betty's reading."

Walking over, her mother discovered that the child was holding the book upside down! Of course, Betty could not read, but she had a mental picture of what it meant to read.

Similarly, boys and girls often play "grown-up." They imitate fire fighters, police officers, or cowboys and recreate adult activities with their teddy bears or dolls. They play doctor and nurse and take turns "healing" one another or their pets.

Language also becomes important at this stage, as children move from infant babbling into a kind of egocentric talking. Many preschoolers begin to talk constantly, paying little or no attention to the listener. The ability to really communicate comes later. For example, every Monday when the cleaning woman, Mrs. Scott, came to Suzy's house, the three-year-old would follow her from room to room, chatting incessantly. Mrs. Scott seemed to know that she wasn't expected to be part of the conversation: her job was to listen. Sometimes Mrs. Scott would find Suzy in one of the rooms, talking to herself, not caring whether or not anyone else could hear her.

I have also seen children at this stage go from person to person, carrying on their own independent dialogue. One little girl talked to four adults in different rooms about her doll. It didn't matter what the adults said, the child ignored them and continued her story. She didn't want a conversation, she simply wanted to talk.

Sensory Development

The first three years of a child's life are the most important for developing language, sensory-motor skills, social skills, and a sense of curiosity. Later, the first three grades in school are the most important years for establishing a foundation for school success. If the "basics" are not established at this point, the child may acquire only partial skills or not pick them up at all.

Jeff, who is now twenty-one years old, is a bright young man and a high school dropout; he didn't pick up the basics at the right time. Jeff can tell me all about the ozone but can't spell the word or many others. He doesn't know phonics and writes in a cramped position, mixing up capital letters with small ones. It is painful to hear him trying to sound out words. He must struggle now to learn the basics, and when he is finished "reading," he doesn't know what he has read.

Intellectual Development

According to Piaget, it takes six or seven years before a child acquires the ability to think in concrete and logical terms.

From age two to about four, most children can build a block tower to knock over; at age five to around seven, that same child begins creating make-believe stories about the tower. One boy, for instance, spent hours making up fantasies in which his favorite TV cartoon hero lived in the tower and fought great battles in and around it.

At about age seven or eight, your child will begin to think "in his head," though he must still rely on concrete and tangible information. Mental manipulation is only possible when applied to information directly experienced by the senses (seen, heard, felt, or experienced).

Studies show that the capacity to absorb new information reaches its peak sometime between the ages of eleven (puberty) and around fifteen (adolescence)—between grades six and ten. In other words, an eleven-year-old often starts to make the transition from the concrete to the abstract.

The fifteen-year-old may begin to go beyond concrete facts into purely symbolic areas, moving from things to ideas. (The development of adolescent intelligence will be discussed in Chapter 8.)

The Dyslexic Child's Learning Pattern

So far, our discussion has been about the intellectual development of children in general. But as I have mentioned, dyslexic children learn differently than nondyslexic children. They remain in the concrete mode of mental operation all their lives. They are called *concrete learners* because they rely heavily on concrete objects as pegs on which to hang ideas. Parents and teachers often complain that these children are scattered or disorganized in their thinking. It is difficult for a dyslexic to focus. They must *learn* how to do what comes so naturally to others: to listen, to follow directions, and to integrate the information in order to follow a specific process. Parents and teachers often complain that the child will compulsively begin a task before he has complete instructions or that the child will begin to write a spelling word before the teacher has finished pronouncing it.

Ordinarily, a child of seven begins to make mental transitions from the concrete to the abstract and by the age of fifteen has moved from concrete to purely symbolic representation; that is, the child can think beyond concrete facts and come to conclusions on a purely intellectual level.

In her biography *A Personal Account of Victory over Dyslexia,* Eileen Simpson says that she thought there was something wrong with her brain. "I seemed to be like other children but I was not like them. I could not learn to read and spell." In teaching herself the alphabet by touch, she stumbled on a way to help herself learn to read. After that, over a period of years, she gained the much sought-after victory.

The human brain is like a great and wonderful powerhouse containing millions upon millions of wires. Just as people depend on the powerhouse for electricity, so we depend on our brains for learning. But just as powerhouses can be wired in different ways—each type of wiring producing a different result—so can our brains be "wired" differently. There is nothing "wrong" with a dyslexic's brain: It is just wired differently. Parents can help a dyslexic child by explaining that his or her way of learning is different from that of other people. The dyslexic child is just as smart as anyone else, but in a different way. The dyslexic child may even be extremely intelligent but have trouble handling abstracts. Here are some specifics.

The dyslexic child is a child of extremes. He can seemingly be overwhelmed by too many people, too much noise, too many sights, and too many changes that make him constantly confused and uncertain. In an effort to organize behavior, the dyslexic child may become rigid, sticking to a single way of doing things. It is impossible for him to see that there are numerous ways to reach the same goal. He becomes inflexible, unable to tolerate any change of routine.

Mary, for example, was taught to set the table in correct order for dinner. When an item, such as a second fork, was not needed, she didn't understand why she should not put it down. She insisted that the table be set in the same way on every occasion and became terribly upset when the order of silverware was changed.

Any child who goes to school each day by the same route will be upset if, on occasion, he or she needs to take a different route. To an already burdened dyslexic child, such a change can be very disturbing.

Dyslexics often lack a sense of humor and can miss the point of a story or metaphor. They interpret symbolic language literally and don't understand such metaphors as "Your father will blow his stack if he hears you," or "It's as plain as the nose on your face," or "This bread is as hard as a rock." They are likely to wonder where the stack is, how something can be like their nose, and how bread can be a rock. To help the dyslexic develop some flexibility in his thinking, you must not only express the metaphor but also explain it. Remind the child that some people take longer to understand, remember, and use information. Once a dyslexic understands his problems and learns to compensate for them, he gains self-esteem and the means to make his life fulfilled and happy.

Intelligence and Social Skills

The development of the intellect and the development of social skills go hand in hand. The dyslexic child's social skills are generally on the level of those of a much younger child. He has difficulty organizing and planning any kind of social gathering.

An older dyslexic child, for example, is still likely to crave center stage, not because of ambition or a sense of power, but because of his immaturity. At a family gathering, this child will get up and start singing at the top of his voice or insist that people pay attention to him regardless of what else those people may be discussing. This developmental lag may be due to a lack of training in early basic skills or to delayed development.

Since the dyslexic operates in the concrete mode all his life, it appears that he especially needs to rehearse standard social skills until they become automatic. He needs to practice—smiling, offering a friendly handshake, or making a pleasant remark. This will be covered in detail in Chapter 7.

You can help your child rehearse social behavior for church, a party, a picnic, or an overnight camping excursion. When the dyslexic becomes an adolescent, however, it becomes more difficult, because at that point, his peers become his mentors.

Immaturity in the Dyslexic Child

Most children seem to move into sequential levels of development naturally and smoothly. The dyslexic child doesn't; he requires more attention, patience, and encouragement than most children. A child who is simply immature will grow out of it in time, but the dyslexic will encounter problems all his life.

It is helpful for you to know the signs of immaturity in a dyslexic child so you can understand the difference between immaturity and dyslexia. Immaturity will be grown out of, but dyslexia will create constant difficulties throughout childhood, adolescence, and adulthood. Ask yourself these questions:

1. Does my child becomc overstimulated by sights and sounds?

2. Does my child seem to react in a disorganized way, perhaps because he can only grasp fragments of what he sees and hears?
3. Does my child have trouble separating one idea, one sound, one symbol from another?
4. Does my child do everything in excess?
5. Does my child have trouble understanding distance and direction?
6. Does my child have trouble understanding the concept of time?
7. Does my child have trouble organizing space for books, papers, toys?
8. Is my child clumsy? Does he often fall, trip, or bump into furniture? Does he seem unsteady on his feet?
9. Does my child react to everything (noise, people, events) at the same time? Does he have trouble focusing on one thing at a time?
10. Does my child seem to jump from one activity or thought to another?

Don't make snap judgments from your answers. Ask yourself these questions several times and observe your child for a while, noting his behavior.

One mother observed her children for several weeks. Her older child, a five-year-old boy, constantly wanted to be the center of attention. When they had visitors, he would often come into the living room and start doing handstands in the corner. He was also extremely disorganized. He couldn't seem to put his toys back on the correct shelves, constantly threw papers on the floor, and had trouble working with his hands.

The other child, a three-year-old boy, was almost the opposite. Despite his age, he was much more organized than his older brother. This confirmed the mother's suspicions that her older son needed some help, but she would not know whether he was dyslexic until he started school and began to read. She first made sure she gave him extra attention and she refrained from comparing his behavior to that of his brother. She then put him in charge of cleaning up his own room each day and took him through the process step-by-step, starting with one toy left out, two toys, and so forth, until he could pick up a number of things without supervision. He also acquired dexterity by practicing with an educational toy (which required that he put different shaped objects into their appropriate holes). By the time the boy reached first grade, he had made considerable improvement.

The Dyslexic Child's Difficulty with Focusing

All children must learn how to focus on a single task, but this is more difficult for some than others, especially dyslexics. This difficulty is now commonly called *attention deficit disorder (ADD)*. Children with this difficulty are often distracted or confused by too much stimulation.

For example, if a child with ADD is told to go to the kitchen and get some butter, he might hear a loud noise on the way to the kitchen, run to the window to see what it is, and forget the butter completely. Or the child might stop listening to his mother or father because he is jumping up and down or watching the dog chase the cat.

Later at school, this is the child who taps his foot on the floor or raps a pencil on the chair. If the disturbance is called to his attention, the child will probably say, "Sorry, I didn't mean to," because he is totally unaware of his actions. This child will constantly jump up to sharpen his pencil (if permitted) or will get a drink or go to the bathroom several times during a lesson. He is easily disturbed and becomes irritable at the slightest contradiction.

His mood swings are frequent and unpredictable. If the child is *hyperactive,* he can't seem to help being restless, unfocused, and in constant motion. Because this child's nervous system is immature, he cannot control sudden changes of behavior. Another type of child, called *hypoactive,* also can't focus well. Hypoactive children, who are withdrawn and shy, manage to escape attention at school and at home. They spend a lot of time playing by themselves or watching television. Because they are so quiet, they are often forgotten. They give no one any trouble. Unfortunately, they themselves are in a lot of trouble. These children have lost their sense of worth, and they live in anxiety and guilt.

Preparing Your Child for School Tasks

Dyslexic children need understanding and support in school and at home to cope with their specific difficulties. You can help your child by explaining what it means to be dyslexic and by reassuring him that it is not something to be ashamed of. Dyslexics possess the same central nervous system and brain structure as all human beings, but they inherit a puzzling difference in the manner in which they process and interpret information.

In addition, learning how to learn presents the dyslexic with special difficulties. Since experience is the key to intellectual development, dyslexics need more opportunities to experience certain skills than children who seem to pick up the skills automatically. At school, in order to understand a certain task, the dyslexic must first learn how to *focus* on the task, then learn how to *do* the task. Sometimes it takes longer to learn how to focus than to learn how to do the task itself.

The dyslexic child's inability to organize makes it difficult for him to make decisions by himself. You will constantly need to support your child in the choices he faces daily: what to eat, what toys to play with, or what to do in free time.

As a result of these problems, a dyslexic child often has great difficulty taking written examinations. Although he may be able to read the questions, he cannot understand which answer would be correct. That is why dyslexics should be permitted to respond to examination questions orally. When responding orally, a dyslexic is not hampered by the difficulty of integrating information that must first be read, then understood, then put in sequential order, and finally written down. We will discuss how to help the dyslexic with this in a later chapter. Below you will find activities you can do with your child at home that will improve the skills he needs for school.

Associating Symbols

Teachers often build a sight vocabulary by associating a child's simple experiences with *sight words,* such as *walk* and *run.* These are usually printed on large index cards and reviewed every day. The children respond by acting out the words. Teachers also review these words with games on the board that give children the opportunity to match action with symbol.

You can do the same thing when your child is three or four years old. Make the cards at home and use them for games. You can also label things and let your child practice associating objects with names. Start with words for things your child sees all the time, such as *dog, cat, car, doll, house, door,* and *bed.*

Later, you can use these words in short sentences—"Walk to the door," "Look at the dog," "Sit on the bed," "Pet the cat"—and ask your child to act out the directions. While they appear simple, these games help build powerful connections for both the dyslexic and the learning-disabled child. You could even hang a small chalkboard in your kitchen on which family members can write instructions and messages or take dictation for spelling, phonic patterns, and other school tasks. One of my favorite memories involves our family chalkboard. Our kitchen had a wall between the pantry and laundry room that my father painted green and made into a chalkboard. As my mother moved about the kitchen preparing a meal, she would snare us into writing answers to questions, adding columns of numbers, and spelling out words or phonic patterns.

Space and Time

The concepts of time and space are important because they form the organizational backbone necessary for any kind of learning. A child uses these abilities when he cleans up his bedroom, sets the table, gets dressed for school, takes timed tests, makes up a schedule, eats lunch or dinner, or goes to bed and gets up. By the time your child enters school, he should feel comfortable in an environment bound by space and time. Let's look at each concept separately.

Introducing Space

Space involves position and place, such as left and right, up and down, in and out, under and over, front and back. Understanding spacial relationships is crucial if a child is to see himself as separate from another and from objects within the environment.

All children have trouble with space initially, but the dyslexic child has special problems. If he doesn't know direction, he probably can't understand that his body has two sides. He also finds it almost impossible to coordinate several parts of the body at the same time into one action. Children with this difficulty are often afraid of large areas and throw tantrums or wander off in the grocery or department store.

Dyslexic children often have a problem with the concept of space when they start kindergarten. They can't draw a straight line, cut out an object, color within lines, or paste anything on drawing paper. Sometimes they can't identify the space they are supposed to stand or sit in. They turn left when the teacher says turn right and right when the teacher says turn left. They will put their names on the left side of the paper when the teacher instructs the class to put it on the right. Sometimes this problem extends well into adulthood.

For instance, as an adult, Mary couldn't draw a straight line. Frequently, she would put her name on the left side of her paper instead of the right and sometimes even at the bottom or in the middle. Mary dreamed of playing the piano, but she kept getting confused and couldn't seem to cross the midline of her body with her fingers. As a result, she became extremely frustrated with anything that required her to master space placement with her hands.

I remember working with a high school student who played basketball well but who was dropped from the team because she often confused the positions of the baskets. When she got the ball, she would run in the opposite direction and dunk the ball in the opposing team's basket.

By about five years of age, most children have developed a sense of their own body and have become clearly right- or left-handed. Still, it is not uncommon for children of five or six to confuse directions or to make mistakes when writing letters, words, and numbers; a delay does not necessarily mean that the child is dyslexic. But if your child continues to have problems that you believe might indicate dyslexia, I encourage you to help him recognize the difference between left and right, up and down, in and out, and other spatial relationships. You can reinforce these lessons by making games of them.

While cooking. Teach taking the pans or dishes in and out of the cupboard, taking the silverware out of the drawer, putting food in the oven.

While playing. Ask your child to turn the toy car or truck left or right, pick it up, put it down. Take a toy and turn it in several directions and have your child tell you whether you have turned it left or right.

While picking up his room. Teach your child to put his toys back in the box and take them out. Ask him to pick his books up off the floor and put them on the shelf. Explain the right and left side of the room; up to the ceiling and down on the floor. Practice saying the words with him.

While driving. Have your child identify left or right as you make left or right turns. Point out different buildings and ask him whether the building is on the left or right side of the road.

A dyslexic child will always have difficulty with directions and must repeat them many times before they become automatic. Once he becomes aware of his position in space, he will be capable of translating this skill onto paper or the board, into artwork, and into games on the school playing field.

Introducing Time

A child's sense of time is primitive; time is relevant only in how it affects his own immediate needs. Gradually, children begin to understand what *wait* and *soon* mean, and later they begin to understand that events take place that affect other people at other times and in other places.

Young children have very little understanding of the past or future. For them everything is now, and time doesn't exist between years. But a child of five will use such words as *yesterday, today,* and *tomorrow.* He can tell you what day follows Sunday and how old he will be on the next birthday. By seven or eight, children can name the months and the seasons of the year and can usually tell time using a clock. For dyslexics, however, the concept of time remains confusing for many years.

I remember a first grader who listened to a classroom guest describe where the president lived and what he did. When the guest asked for questions, the little girl raised her hand and announced that her father was in Washington, too. Actually the little girl's classroom was in a Los Angeles school and her father worked in that city. But he *had* worked in Washington several years ago and to her, then was now.

In another example, Russ, a teenager, had absolutely no sense of time. At about eleven o'clock on Sunday night, he would jump up and rush to the department store to buy a tie. He would rush to the bank and expect to find everyone there at three o'clock in the morning. He would show up for class at the crack of dawn. He would be puzzled when he turned on the television and failed to find his favorite program. Although these may seem extreme examples, I assure you, they aren't; many dyslexic children have these problems. Time is especially crucial and especially difficult for the dyslexic and often provides clues for detecting learning problems. A "long time," "less time," and "more time" have no meaning for the dyslexic child. Scolding him for his lack of understanding only reinforces the idea that he is out of step with everyone and does everything wrong.

One of my former students, Jim, couldn't seem to get up in the morning. He could never find his shoes or his schoolbooks and he never had time to eat. At school, he always went through the classroom row by row before he found his desk, and then he simply dumped his books and jacket on top of the desk and sat down.

This continued until Jim's mother and I got together to work out a solution. His mother developed a system so he could get up in the morning, have time for a good breakfast, find his schoolbooks, and get to school on time. I marked the way to his desk on the floor with tape. Jim learned to put his books on a shelf and hang up his jacket in the cloakroom. He was required to follow each of these steps every day until he established some order in his life.

Because a dyslexic child has no sense of order or sequence, he can't name the days of the week or seasons of the year or count or recite the alphabet. A child who is a concrete learner actually needs to see what he is counting (jars, apples, money) before he can form a mental picture. His sense of time is primitive, and he tends to associate time with important events or life experiences (the night of the big wind, harvesttime, the day Jim broke his leg) rather than with words. Because it is impossible to display segments of time physically—that is, you can't place a bunch of minutes or days on the table—the dyslexic child gets very confused. However, you can introduce your young child to the concept of time early in the following ways.

Clock time. Point out that life is broken into segments of time. Ask your child whether he knows the *numerical* time at which certain events occur, like bedtime, naptime, or dinnertime.

Purchase or make a clock face and teach him what the numbers designate and why the hands move at different speeds.

Teach minutes using a minute hourglass. Have your child turn the hourglass upside down. Tell him it takes one minute for the sand to run from the top to the bottom. Show him what this means on the clock face. Set an egg timer for five minutes, then have him set the timer and show him what this means on the clock face.

Calendar time. Some parents make a project out of constructing their own calendar, creating it in the form of a bear's face, a teakettle, or something else familiar to their child. A child is more likely to learn if the learning tools are fun and personal.

Tell your child about the seasons and explain what makes one season different from another. Ask him to cut out pictures from a magazine that show spring, summer, fall, and winter and paste them in a large scrapbook.

Talk to him about such holidays as Christmas, Halloween, and Easter and have him learn what season these holidays occur in. Ask him to cut out pictures of these holidays from magazines and place them where they belong on your calendar.

Give him a large box of crayons and ask him to pick out the colors he associates with spring (pastel pinks and yellows), summer (bright reds and blues), fall (browns, oranges, dark yellows), and winter (blacks, whites, dark purples). Ask him to draw pictures of winter, summer, spring, and fall using his crayons.

Your dyslexic child needs lots of practice to grasp and understand both space and time. Keep working with him until he can automatically point left and right and up and down and until he understands what you say when you tell him "We will go in five minutes," or "You will get presents at Christmas." This kind of practice goes a long way toward helping him understand space and time as life concepts.

3

Parenting the Dyslexic Child

> Children can grow only in an environment of unconditional love.
>
> —*Eileen M. Cronin*

A family fulfills its obligation in the true sense when the needs of every member are met, when positive relationships are created, and when each person is supported in love and serenity. The family plays a vital part in helping a dyslexic child to learn, to grow, and to fit happily into a social system where he receives guidance and direction. Only in an atmosphere of unconditional love and acceptance are children free to develop their uniqueness and blossom into the special human beings they are meant to be. In his book *The Family: A Revolutionary Way of Self-Discovery,* John Bradshaw says: "The first ten years of life are those most influenced by patterns of behavior and relationships set up in the home which predict what kind of persons children will become as adults. Children learn first and best from the lived messages of their family rather than from words of direction or explanation."

I also believe that children are primarily influenced by how parents treat them, rather than by what parents tell them. A child who is greeted with a smile and hugged with warmth learns to love himself and becomes capable of trusting others.

Charlie's mother and father, for example, made it a habit to help others. Every Saturday, his father mowed the lawn of an elderly widow who lived across the street, who couldn't afford to hire someone and didn't have the strength to do it herself. Charlie's mother often brought groceries to a needy family in the neighborhood and shopped weekly for a bedridden neighbor. As Charlie grew older, he accepted this "lived message" as a way of life; and because he was constantly helping others, he was both well known and well liked throughout the neighborhood.

A sense of being loved can be crucial when a child is developing early skills. For example, a little boy of four who was "helping" his grandfather in the backyard one day stopped for a moment to look up and say, "I love you, Grandpa." Overwhelmed, his grandfather replied, "I love you too, Sammy." The little boy knew he was loved and so did his grandfather! They had both learned a lesson that day.

Although Sammy had had learning difficulties during his early years, he knew he was loved at home and was confident that he could do almost anything he set his sights on. He overcame his difficulties, went on to college, and eventually became a successful network newscaster. Later, when he was asked how he had overcome his learning problems, he credited both his grandfather and his family. "It started with my grandfather's love," he told his interviewer. "That was all I needed to have the confidence to tackle any problem and overcome any difficulty. And hopefully, I've been able to transfer this love and this confidence to my own children."

What Is Parenting?

The family structures in which children are being raised today are much more varied than they used to be. Although there are still two-parent households, often both parents must go to work and leave their children in a child-care facility. There are also more single-parent households headed by women.

It is especially difficult to raise children in a single-parent household—to be a full-time mom or dad at home as well as a full-time worker outside the home. Whatever the obstacles, you must make the home the center of your family's life. Children never forget parental influences as they grow into adulthood.

One well-known sports star, for instance, constantly talks about the days his mother worked in a local factory five days a week, then spent the weekends cleaning offices just to support him and his two brothers. "We lived in a poor part of town," he explains, "since that is all we could afford. But I have great memories of the neighbors, nights on the roof watching the stars, playing basketball out back with other kids, and excursions around the city with my mother."

He also talks about passing clothes down from one brother to another and sometimes freezing in the winter because they couldn't afford to heat their apartment. These were hard times, yet he cherishes the memories because he knew his mother loved him. "I will never forget those days," he says, "and in some ways they were the best of my life. My mother is gone now, but she helped make all three of us successful."

In her book *Family: The Center of Formation,* Marjorie Johnson says that family members need to encourage the goodness and giftedness they see in one another. Parents need to focus on what their children can achieve rather than what they expect them to achieve. It is important to accept each child's uniqueness and talents for exactly what they are. Each child needs to feel secure and worthwhile, loved at home and accepted in school, in order to do his best. A child who seems different or is dyslexic is just as uniquely gifted as any other child. Parents must patiently help this child through the rough times at home and in school.

Parenting the dyslexic child is, in general, no different from parenting any other child. Dyslexic children go through the same growth pattern common to all children, but because maturation is often delayed, parents often find this period extremely challenging and stressful. Although dyslexic children are usually of normal intelligence—often even gifted—they sometimes behave as if they were mentally slow or developmentally immature. Dispositions, of course, also vary tremendously. Some dyslexic children are outgoing and sensitive toward others, despite their difficulties, while others become shy and reflective. The outgoing or disruptive child has no trouble getting attention, but the shy child can be easily forgotten in a busy home, especially if both parents work.

The Shy Child

Parents must remind themselves and others to include the shy child, making sure that he gets as much attention as his brothers and sisters. I will go into more detail about the specific things you can do to help your shy dyslexic child later in this chapter, in the section on group participation.

Family Life and Humor

When the pressures of life become too great, all families need some sort of a relief valve. If a family can see the funny side of a situation and laugh together, the burden lifts and they become bonded in understanding and optimism. The following scenario illustrates how helpful humor can be in a family with a dyslexic child.

Doris, a mother of four, makes sure that her children always see the funny side of a mistake. When her six-year-old was first assigned to set the table, he insisted on placing three spoons at each plate rather than a knife, fork, and spoon. Instead of scolding him, as some parents might, Doris saw the funny side and treated it as a correctable mistake. She hugged him and explained how difficult it would be to eat with just spoons . . . and together they laughed at what he had done. Then with great seriousness, they set the table correctly together. And although the boy continued to set the table incorrectly for several weeks, they always had a laugh over it, and the boy eventually rectified his mistake.

Another family established what they called their "after-dinner skit." Whenever a child was rude, brought home poor grades, or failed to clean up his room, he was required to put on a skit for the whole family after dinner. One night, three of the children acted out the Three Little Pigs. It was so funny that the whole room exploded in laughter, and after that, the children's skits were always silly. They helped create a wonderful mood of cooperation. Laughter helps parents—and children—over the difficult hurdles of mistakes, disappointments, and setbacks.

As Sally Smith says in *No Easy Answers,* the use of humor and the absurd can be effective tools for discipline, teaching, and testing. A school or home where laughter abounds among members is usually a place where children are given many opportunities to enjoy learning and living. Dyslexic children do have difficulties, some more serious than others, and these difficulties do require serious attention, yet nothing dispels an atmosphere of anxiety faster than laughter.

This is not to imply that all situations require a light touch. Parents and teachers know that all dilemmas are not funny. Negative or inappropriate behavior at home or in school should never be rewarded with laughter.

In general, a sense of the absurd can put a problem or mistake in perspective, for parents as well as for children and teachers. It is important to remember that you don't have to know everything. By admitting your own mistakes, you convey an important message to children: Everyone can learn from mistakes.

Family Participation and Responsibility

We all expect structure in our personal life; the dyslexic child must learn that there is structure and responsibility in his family life and that he is expected to participate in the family duties shared by all members. He might be assigned to bring in the paper every night, set the table, or do some other simple chore.

Setting the table provides an excellent lesson in sequence—first the plates, then the silver, then the glasses, then the napkins. You will, of course, have to repeat this process several times before the child can set the table with ease and confidence.

One family rotates chores among the three children and parents. One child dries and puts away the dishes for three or four days; then that chore rotates to another child. The chores the children do include mowing the lawn, weeding the flower beds, dusting the furniture, and setting the table. In addition, they put one member in charge of seeing that chores are completed each week.

Group Participation

Usually as children grow up, they progress from playing with one or two playmates to playing with many playmates, eventually becoming a member of a group. But because of his immaturity and school failures, the dyslexic child is rarely chosen to participate in such school activities as games, parties, or other class affairs.

Remember the fifth-grade boy I mentioned in Chapter 1, who wandered the school yard alone at recess and lunchtime with a book under his arm? The other children never picked him to be on their teams and seldom talked to him out of class. He couldn't read, but by carrying a book, he tried to convey the message that he was no different from the kids in the class—that he, too, could read. He sensed that the ability to read meant acceptance in the classroom, in the school yard, and in life.

Parents of a dyslexic child must be aware of the possible rejection and isolation he suffers and devise strategies to help him participate in games, parties, and other fun occasions. You might invite other children over to play. Also, you could help him become more proficient in areas that interest him, so that other children will recognize his abilities. One father, who saw that his son had trouble playing soccer, practiced with him for weeks until he could play an acceptable game. Within a few more weeks, the boys at school, who played regularly, welcomed the child into their games.

In another case, a child's mother set up a complete playground of slides, swings, and a jungle gym in the backyard. She then invited the neighbors and their children for a Saturday barbecue and open house and let the children know that they were always welcome. As a result, her child had plenty of playmates.

Professional Help

To help their children cope, parents sometimes need to seek professional assistance. Dyslexia is a very complex phenomenon, but fortunately the understanding of dyslexia among psychologists, psychiatrists, and medical experts has grown remarkably in the last few years. (See Appendix G, "Support Groups," for a list of associations and other qualified resources.)

Depending on the degree of their disability, some dyslexic children may also suffer from a behavior disorder as well. Occasionally, it is necessary to refer a dyslexic child who is hyperactive or hypoactive to either medical or psychological help, or both. Whether or not you seek help depends to what extent the child is suffering from depression, low self-esteem, or other behavior disorders.

Research has shown that certain stimulant drugs such as Ritalin and Dexedrine work wonders for hyperactive children, making them calmer and less active, so that they can concentrate and learn. These drugs enable the children to filter overstimulating situations. Children generally need these drugs only until their responses mature to the point that they can control the messages coming into the brain, generally around puberty or adolescence.

A professional should be able to answer any question clearly and simply, in terms you can understand. If a professional is vague or speaks too technically, you will probably not be able to establish a good relationship. You and your child must be able to communicate well with your doctor or therapist, on a level you can all understand. If you find that this is not happening, look for someone in whom you can have confidence.

Case Study

Bruce, Age 9, Grade 3
Mother: Sally, Age 26
Father: Tom, Age 35
Sister: Susan, Age 7

Reason for Referral Problems with reading, writing, and mathematics. Has a short attention span and poor control of temper.

Mother Bruce was a happy, inquisitive youngster during his first three years. Although we live in a suburban neighborhood with lots of children, Bruce doesn't want to play with any of them. Two years ago, Bruce's dad installed a swing set in the backyard, but though Bruce and Susan, his sister, play on it a lot, none of the neighborhood kids ever join them.

Susan is just two years younger than Bruce, but they are not close. After we brought Susan home, Bruce demanded more attention. If I was feeding the baby, he'd bring a toy and demand I play with him, or if I were changing her diapers, he would tug at my arm until I paid attention to him. I'm afraid I didn't show much patience with him during those years.

Bruce and Susan argue a lot. Sometimes I have to play referee. Since I usually side with Susan, Bruce stalks off into his room and refuses to come out. At other times, Bruce ignores his sister and that hurts her feelings.

He was always talkative around us, but when I took him into groups of people, he became upset and wanted to leave. In the beginning, I invited other children here to play, but Bruce just disappeared into a shell. I recognized then that he was terribly shy and a loner, but I just assumed he'd get along when we put him in nursery school.

I never worried about him because he seemed bright and creative. He was always asking questions about how things work and often seemed to understand without asking. Once he pointed at the blades on the lawn mower and then at the grass. He understood how it worked. I thought that was pretty bright for a child not yet three.

When Bruce turned three, Tom and I decided to put him in nursery school so I could go to work to supplement the family income. The minute we walked in the door, he shut up and wouldn't talk to the other kids. When the teacher knelt down to talk to him, he put his hands over his face and hid behind me. When I tried to leave, he clung to me and screamed at the top of his lungs.

We repeated this scene three times. Finally, the principal told me I should take him home and enjoy him. She said that they just weren't equipped to handle this type of child. The minute we walked out the door, he became happy and talkative again. At home he seemed outgoing and normal.

About six months later, we enrolled Bruce in another nursery school. He went without a fuss this time, but he never seemed to get anything out of it. Mostly, he just watched the other kids. When I asked if he was having a good time, he always told me no.

When Bruce started first grade, his teacher spent a great deal of extra time with him. She used cards that required him to handle the letters; then she had him make words using the letter cards. He started to make progress, but she left at the end of the first semester and the two teachers who took over insisted on teaching sight words and phonics only.

They also tried to make Bruce play games with the other kids during recess. This backfired and he withdrew further into his shell.

Soon Bruce dropped behind and stopped learning. During the first semester of the first grade, he could sound some letters and recognize a number of words, but during the second semester he seemed to forget everything. Both teachers complained that he wouldn't cooperate. One told me he was probably retarded and just couldn't learn. At times, Bruce became frustrated, screamed, and threw his book. Because of this, our family physician put him on Ritalin. That seemed to calm him down. We also put him under the care of an educational psychologist.

Second grade was more of the same. His teacher told me he would become confused, stumble on every word, and take forever to read a sentence. The kids teased him about his reading. I tried to help him at home, but I seemed to make it worse. He loved to hear me read, but when I would hand him the book and ask him to read, he would throw it across the room.

As he dropped further behind, he became very unhappy and started avoiding everybody. Sometimes I would find him sulking in his room. At that time, we enrolled him in a private clinic where he goes for therapy three times a week. I'm not sure this is helping.

Sometimes I wonder if we are partially at fault. It almost seems like we passed on this problem to Bruce. Neither his father nor I were really good students. I had trouble keeping up from the sixth grade on. But as an adult I seem to have grown out of it and do a lot of reading, mostly romance novels, which I guess is a form of escape from reality. Bruce's father hoped he would be a good student and like school. It's obvious now that Bruce needs a great deal of help from our family.

We're determined to give our son the best education possible. Neither Tom and I are discouraged. We know our son is smart enough, and as far as we're concerned, we're going to give him all the support we can.

Psychologist When Bruce and his mother came into the office, it was immediately clear that he didn't want to be here. Ordinarily, I try to put children at ease by talking about their family, their toys, and their pets. I had tested a seven-year-old just before Bruce arrived, who talked about her kitty for almost ten minutes. In contrast, Bruce sat with his eyes averted and mumbled one- or two-word answers to my questions. He appeared bored and disinterested in the whole process.

Bruce, however, is actually a bright youngster with a better-than-average IQ. Unfortunately, he not only has a severe learning problem, which I believe was aggravated by the school system, but he's psychologically much younger (five or six) than his chronological age (nine).

Despite attempts by his mother to help him be social, Bruce has always remained a loner. At one time, he seemed willing to reach out to other children, but now he is withdrawn and in group activities always remains a spectator.

His mother expressed concern, at an early age, that he was poorly coordinated and was prone to throw temper tantrums, but he also seemed so bright and inquisitive that she decided he would grow out of it by the time he reached kindergarten. His failure to adapt to nursery school should have been a signal that Bruce needed help, but neither the father nor mother connected this reaction with future learning problems. They were more concerned with his social problems.

Once in school, his inability to keep up with the other students aggravated his problems. The impatience of his teachers and the teasing of the other children convinced him that he was dumb and incapable of learning. At this point, he was caught in a trap.

By the time Bruce was referred for evaluation, he was far behind his class and unable to do classroom work on even a first-grade level. More important, he has become preoccupied with failure and blames himself for everything. He is bored, discouraged, and dissatisfied with himself.

In the office, I administered a standard battery of tests that would evaluate Bruce's self-esteem, his psychological age, his visual memory, and his fine-motor coordination. Children need fine-motor coordination to draw, color with crayons, cut with scissors, and write with pens or pencils.

Once he started working on the tests, he erased and rewrote every answer before moving on to the next one. It was obvious that, although he wanted to keep the whole process at arm's length, he was unsure and anxious about his performance.

One of the tests that I always ask these youngsters to take is the Draw-a-Man test. This test indicates a child's psychological age and his or her psychosexual development. Some children draw a very complete man and woman, with all the details in place, including hands, ears, and feet. Many draw men in pants and with short hair, women with a dress and long hair.

Bruce drew two small, helpless, almost stick figures. It was impossible to tell which was the man and which was the woman. Bruce shows little awareness of the differences between boys and girls and exhibits extremely low self-esteem. Although I believe he is intelligent enough to achieve grade level, he will need several years of remedial treatment.

Evaluating Teacher I wish we could have started working on Bruce's learning problems several years ago. His initial failure has created an image problem that has gotten progressively worse.

Despite four full years of public school, including kindergarten, he is still struggling to learn the basic elements of reading and writing. Some children learn best by seeing the words and letters, others do well when they hear them, and some need to manipulate the words and letters with their hands.

Bruce learns best by working with his hands (*kinesthetic*). His visual learning skills are especially poor. Part of this may be a physical problem. He cannot seem to follow a letter card moved up and down in front of him. He has special problems tracking an object, and his peripheral vision is extremely poor. He also can't tolerate looking at anything that spins or rotates.

His initial first-grade teacher seemed to understand that Bruce needed to learn by using his hands. By helping him work with letter cards, and by having him place the cards in front of him to form words, he made normal progress. When this was stopped, all learning stopped.

The more difficulty he had, the more depressed he seemed to get. His teachers reported that he often got angry when they asked him to read, and sometimes a reading session would end with Bruce throwing his book across the room. The other students weren't very helpful. They teased him mercilessly about his reading, often mocking him at recess and making him feel like an outcast.

By the time we first saw Bruce, he no longer wanted to even try. He blamed himself for his problem and decided that he'd never be like the other kids. In testing Bruce, however, we discovered he could reason quite well and performed above average on our general performance and verbal test that we use to establish a child's IQ.

In our tests, we found that he still couldn't color within the lines, draw a straight line with a pencil, or make a recognizable letter A. This indicates a fine-motor coordination problem that makes writing difficult. His main problems showed up on the visual tests. He couldn't visually perceive or identify letters and words, he couldn't look at a word and write it down (visual-motor coordination), and he couldn't identify sounds or recognize sight words.

It was clear that Bruce needed to work on improving his visual skills. We recommended that he receive additional auditory and visual training with words and letters. We also suggested that since he initially learned by working with letters and words on cards, that he be given supplemental kinesthetic-tactile exercises.

Bruce also needs to bolster his self-esteem so that he will feel comfortable tackling new projects and reaching out to other children. As long as he won't try, he will never reach grade level.

The Follow-up Fortunately, Bruce's parents understood that many of his problems stemmed from his feelings about himself as well as from his learning problems. They also realized that since he was psychologically immature, he would have a problem controlling his temper for many years.

As a result of the recommendations, Bruce's parents enrolled him in a remedial program in a private school that would provide both social and academic training. During his fourth year, Bruce made considerable progress; by the end of that year, he reached the second-grade level. He currently has a third-grade vocabulary, has improved his spelling skills, and has a much better comprehension of what he reads. His current teachers are tremendously encouraged and feel he can catch up to grade level within the next few years.

4

Help at School

> The dyslexic is a concrete learner. He begins with the conclusion and works backward.
>
> —*Eileen M. Cronin*

All parents know that unless their child masters the skills of language—speaking, reading, and writing—he or she will have problems fitting into school and into society.

The school should be more than an institution or system that imparts knowledge or a place where students attain mastery in reading, writing, spelling, and math. A school should also be a place that offers help and support to any learning-disabled child. The dyslexic child, especially, needs understanding and support. You and your child's teacher must be convinced that your child can learn, even though he may learn in a different manner and at a different speed from others. Your objective should be to discover how your child learns and how to design ways to teach your child to learn more effectively—ideally with his teacher's assistance. Some clues to understanding how your child learns can be found in the way he speaks, behaves, and works; in his interests and talents; in the results of formal school tests; in the teacher's records; and in your own and the teacher's observations.

When you begin to see signs that your child is having trouble, you need to get as much assistance as you can from the school. By testing, the school can help you determine whether your child is dyslexic; some schools offer remedial help. Your child's teacher might also gear the teaching program to make learning easier for him. Of course, you can't demand that teachers give your child special training, but they can discuss his problem, observe how much real help he is getting, and determine what assistance you need to provide at home.

The Parent-Teacher Conference

After you have answered the questions below, make an appointment with your child's teacher. The questions are designed to give you a starting point for a frank discussion with the teacher.

Respond to the questions honestly, making notes of your answers.

1. Does my child know the days of the week?
2. Does my child understand the words *up, down, behind, over, under, left,* and *right* as they are given in directions ("Put your name at the top right-hand side of your paper")?
3. Is my child organized? Does he lose his coat, lunch, books, or homework? Does he have a messy desk or messy work papers? Does he consistently have trouble finding things?
4. Is my child lazy? Is he overactive?
5. Does my child have an unusual number of good days and bad days? Are his mood swings unpredictable?

6. Does my child have a short attention span?
7. Does my child constantly forget things he should remember? In particular, does he forget what familiar words should look like when written?
8. Does my child print or write slowly and laboriously? Is he clumsy when walking or running?
9. Does he daydream? Act silly? Repeat words or actions over and over?
10. Does he seem distracted when someone reads a story or explains a math process?
11. Does he have a low tolerance level for mistakes?

Once you have discussed these questions with the teacher, you will both have a better understanding of your child's behavior and abilities. Using your answers as a basis, you can now move on to more general questions of your child's personality and learning patterns. To do this detective work properly, both you and the teacher should center your concern and help for your child around his pattern of learning.

1. What strengths does the child have? What does he remember best?
2. How does he learn best? (Remember, some children are visual learners; others learn best when they hear someone talk about something; still others learn through physical feeling.)
3. What are the child's interests, talents, and hobbies?
4. What does the child like to do? What does he not like to do?
5. Does the child behave inappropriately?
6. As this child's parent or teacher, am I prepared to explain the child's problem to the principal, teachers, doctors, or academic or medical therapists?

Often from this information, you and the teacher can discover your child's unique style of learning and put together a learning situation in the class and at home that allows him to make real progress. This is, of course, the ideal situation. In reality, I'm afraid, many teachers don't want to—or can't—take the time to give such individual attention to a child.

A parent should still take the time to schedule an appointment and discuss the problem in as much detail as possible. To make progress at this point, the dyslexic child needs additional help both at school and at home.

A dyslexic once said to me that she never learned anything in school . . . what a sad indictment.

Test Results

Your child's periodic class test results will tell you and the teacher how he compares with other children according to age and grade. Some schools regularly administer standardized tests taken by children nationally, but I find that teacher-originated tests more accurately reflect the abilities of an individual class or child. These tests evaluate what the teacher has actually taught according to grade objectives; they tend to be a good assessment of a child's progress.

Level of Foundation Skills

Ask your child's teacher whether he or she has kept notes on how well or how poorly your child learns a particular skill. Once you both know what skills are missing, you can ask the teacher to incorporate the necessary repetition of basic skills into the child's regular assignments.

If the teacher cooperates, then you can become involved with homework assignments or other activities at home that reinforce the teacher's curriculum. You will need to persist until your child acquires the necessary *foundation skills* (speech, writing, reading, and math). Without this repetition, your child is in danger of repeating failure, losing interest in school, perhaps eventually dropping out. There are already far too many high school dropouts—and many times, their problem is the lack of basic skills, such as the ability to read.

Finally, you and the teacher need to determine the answers to the following, using the other information you've gathered. Keep these questions in mind as you consider each skill (speech, reading, writing, and math) individually.

1. What does the child know? (foundation skills)
2. What doesn't the child know? (foundation skills)
3. What does the child need to know? (grade objectives)
4. What goals should be set for this child?

Speech

Speech is obviously an important learning skill. It allows us to communicate with each other. We need to be able to ask questions, understand answers, listen to orders and directives, comprehend stories, and respond to complaints.

Dyslexics often have difficulty with sequence when telling stories, as the example of Billy illustrates. Billy loved to talk in front of the class. He always got a big laugh, because his stories were always bizarre. Once he told the class about the birth of his baby brother. According to him, his family played with the baby at home before his mother went to the hospital to give birth, and when it was born, the baby was bigger than Billy. These kinds of mix-ups are typical of dyslexics.

When some learning-handicapped children tell a story, they start somewhere in the middle, at the end, or at a point that is completely unclear to the listener; they can't tell what should come first, second, or third.

Many dyslexics have problems following sequences of events, dates, or numbers; this lack of order is often reflected in the way they approach most school tasks. Since dyslexics can't organize their thoughts, they can't organize their schoolwork or follow the development of an idea. As you can imagine, this is very frustrating and may be the reason their behavior is often unacceptable in school, on the playground, or at home.

You should ask the teacher if your child has had problems telling or understanding stories. It is important to recognize when a child is beginning to fail to recognize words. It is also important for you to know whether the teacher is trying alternative ways to reach the child.

As mentioned previously, some children learn best verbally, others visually, others emotionally or physically. In my work with dyslexic children, I have discovered that children who can't answer written questions easily often do quite well when these same questions are asked orally. If this is the case with your child, try to arrange for opportunities at school and at home for him to talk about his experiences. Sometimes teachers will permit a dyslexic child to take his exams orally.

One third-grade teacher who had three bizarre spellers in her class decided to experiment by letting these children spell the words aloud. As a result, the children's test results improved remarkably. If the teacher is unwilling to take the time to do this, you should try the technique at home. If you find that it works, ask the teacher to let the child spell words orally whenever it doesn't interfere with regular classtime.

Math

Not all children who have problems deciphering words for reading or spelling have trouble with arithmetic, which makes it difficult to recognize dyslexia and puzzling to analyze.

The dyslexic, however, will sometimes show an inflexibility that prevents him from switching easily from one skill to another; for example, he may not be able to move easily from addition to subtraction to multiplication.

As with spelling, verbal math questions are sometimes more easily understood than written equations or word problems. Try asking your child to figure out math problems aloud. If you find that it works, try to encourage his teacher to do so as well.

Also, after you or the teacher has instructed the child to perform an activity, ask him to repeat the instructions. This way, you can be sure that the child understands what he is supposed to do before he does it. (Many children fail examinations because they either hear or read the directions incorrectly.) One teacher I knew got in the habit of saying to his class:

"I am going to tell you about . . ."

"Now I am going to tell you what I told you . . ."

"Now you tell me what I told you."

"Now go and do what I told you."

Writing

Writing is almost impossible for some dyslexics. The concentration they must give to forming letters and keeping them aligned consumes all their energy and attention. As a consequence, they can never finish an assignment within a designated time limit. "Never finished, never right" makes school a dull and unpleasant place for any child.

In my early years of teaching, I dictated spelling words too fast for one dyslexic boy, who had to struggle to keep up with the class. Two or three days of frustration were too much for Bill, a sixth grader: He threw his pencil down at the dictation of the third word and stormed out of the room, saying, "I can't stand this. I hate spelling." I had to learn that it was better for Bill to spell every other word. Spacing the words out gave him the time he needed to hear the word, process its meaning, organize the sequence of letters, "see" the word as a whole in his mind, and order his muscles to write it.

Reading

It is helpful for you or the teacher to have a *reading-learning profile* of your child. Only when you have an accurate profile of skills and goals can you direct the child appropriately. Give your child the profile test below.

Understanding the alphabet. First, evaluate the child's ability to identify and sound out letters. If he doesn't know the symbols (the letters of the alphabet) used to form words and the sounds they designate, he will be unable to read or write. You or a tutor can administer this test easily and informally. Make sure you do not have a reference chart of the alphabet visible during the test.

1. Ask the child how many letters there are in the alphabet; then have him recite them.
2. Print each letter on a square of cardboard (about three inches by three inches). Show them one at a time in mixed order to the child. Have him name each letter.
3. Ask the child to give the sound of each letter as he picks up the card.
4. Mix up the cards and ask the child to write or print each letter after you show it to him.
5. Ask the child to write or print the alphabet, in sequence, from memory.

Word discrimination skills. Word discrimination is the crux of any poor reader's problem. *Sight words* should be recognized automatically and accurately. (You can find lists of sight words and "problem words" in Appendixes B and C.)

1. Print or write sight words and problem words on three-by-five-inch cards.
2. Show each card to the child, maintaining the same rhythm of arm movement (slow, medium, or fast). If he hesitates or starts to sound out the word letter by letter, put it aside and review it later.

Do not permit the child to sound out sight words. He must recognize them spontaneously.

Phonic skills. The words the child misses in the word discrimination test offer a clue to the level of his phonic ability. You can get more detailed information from the test below.

1. Ask the child whether he knows the short and long sounds of vowels.
2. Ask him the sounds of consonants.
3. Does he know special sounds (*oi/oy, aw/au, ou/ow, ph/gh, th/sh, ch/wh*)?
4. Does he recognize these for spelling as well as for reading?

Reading comprehension. Reading is a process. Once the child easily and accurately recognizes words, he will be able to put them together in meaningful context. He must, however, be taught how to do this. Even though your child may recognize words, he will probably not be able to understand their meanings automatically when he reads them in sentences. *Reading comprehension* is a skill that has to be taught.

Skills for comprehension include understanding the following:

The main idea

Details

Inference

Cause and effect

Summarization

The results of a reading skills test will give you a good appraisal of a child's reading ability. The big question for you and the teacher is: Once the child recognizes words, how well does he put these words together to form sentences and paragraphs into meaningful units for understanding? If he can do this, then the child can read. (Chapter 6 explains what questions to ask the child, and it offers ways to help the child obtain comprehension ability.)

The above profile test of reading skills is arranged according to specific goals by grade level. Therefore, you can compare your child's level of achievement with the list to find out what children in his grade can do. If your child is below grade level, you can outline those skills that need to be reinforced, then use the instructions and exercises provided in Chapter 6.

Reading, writing, and spelling foundation skills are absolutely essential before real learning can take place on any level. This might be a short-term goal, if preskills need to be learned, or a long-term goal, if a child is ready to move on to a higher level of skills.

Motivation

Ignatio, one of my sixth-grade pupils, once told me that the best book he ever read was *The Three Little Pigs.* He told me that he had read it seven times! It didn't matter to Ignatio—and I learned it didn't matter to me—that he was a sixth grader reading a primary-grade book. The point was that he could read. He knew the words and understood the story. He was proud of himself. He could read! The moral of this story is that children like to do the things they can do. If they can read something they enjoy, they will read more. Ignatio eventually became an avid reader.

Nobody learns without motivation, and there is no better motivation than success. Learning-disabled children need to be programmed for success every step of the way, and you can help make learning a pleasure. Isn't that what teaching is all about? Hearing "I can do it!" or "I like this!" from a struggling child is a sweet reward for a patient teacher or a proud parent.

The Importance of Structure

Both at home and at school, all children need the security of structure, especially the learning-handicapped child. He needs to know what to do, when to do it, and how to do it. Having a structural framework will allow him to be successful until he is able to become self-directed and independent. For the dyslexic child, *routine* is the backbone of structure.

For example, I remember when the door to the classroom wouldn't open and the small group of learning-handicapped children had to use a room across the hall. When the custodian finally fixed the door, the children were permitted to return. One little boy breathed a sigh of obvious relief and said, "Now we can go back to our own letter boxes!" Others expressed relief that they would now have their own desks, that they knew where to hang their coats, that the clock was where they expected to find it, and that the other details were familiar. Familiarity is important to all children, but especially to dyslexic children.

One third-grade teacher developed a daily routine in which all classroom activities—reading, storytelling, art, and math—occurred in the same sequence and at a designated time. By the second week, the children knew what to expect every minute of the day and began to prepare for each activity ahead of time; that is, for art, they would get out their art supplies and have them ready at exactly the right time. Once a substitute teacher began to handle the day's activities in a random manner, even though she had been given the schedule. At first, she got only a few muttered protests from some of the more aggressive children. But when she failed to start the reading session on time, the whole room exploded. One eight-year-old girl broke into tears and threw her book on the floor; another ran out of the room screaming.

Although most children do not require such stringent adherence to structure, learning-handicapped children absolutely do. These children also need the security of knowing how to enter a room at home or at school, how to greet one another, where their supplies are kept, how to put materials away, and other school-related details. They must learn routines step-by-step until they master them and until organization becomes a habit. You should expect the teacher to provide such routines for any child having trouble in school.

The difficulties the dyslexic child experiences in learning revolve around how he perceives the environment and his inability to make suitable connections. Very young children learn by physically experiencing the differences in objects: seeing them, smelling them, feeling them, and even tasting them. Dyslexic children continue to learn this way because of their sense of concreteness. Learning, of course, means doing more than one thing at once: It means making suitable connections and simultaneously plugging them in.

Evaluating the School Program

Sometimes the school doesn't diagnose the dyslexic child or doesn't have a program to help him. Sometimes the teacher doesn't understand the problem or has established a single program that she adheres to for all students.

A dyslexic child, however, always needs special help. A child who experiences failure in school is usually an unhappy child, and he needs all the understanding parents and teachers can give. To ensure this, you need to become a committed advocate for your child. After your initial contacts with the school and the teacher, you should evaluate the kind of help you can expect from your child's school. You can then decide what more you need ask. Below are some questions to help you.

1. Does the school have the services necessary to help my child?
2. Is his teacher prepared to act as a liaison between me and my child and the administration, other teachers, and the students?
3. Do I believe that the teacher has the courage to step forward and be an advocate for my child?

4. Is this teacher prepared to help the school administration understand my child's dilemma and that of other dyslexic children?
5. Do I believe my child's teacher has enough information about dyslexia to make a suitable referral to a tutor for my child? If not, does he or she know where to go for the answers?
6. Do I feel the teacher will have the patience to give my child extra help? Will he or she be able to take the time necessary for my child? (Note: Teachers as a rule have little time in a busy school day to take on extra remedial work, but they should have information about extra assistance that is available.)
7. Do I feel this teacher knows how to set up a structure for a dyslexic child? Does he or she know the techniques of classroom management that will help my child and other children with learning difficulties?

Hints for Giving Instructions and Explanations

When giving instructions or explanations to children, parents and teachers often forget that they use too many words and that they talk far too fast. How many times have you told a child to do something, only to find that by the time you've finished he is completely lost and can't remember even one thing you've said?

A dyslexic child, especially, can't deal with a lot of words because he has to make an extreme effort to hear, understand, integrate, remember, and then attempt to carry out instructions.

Teachers, in general, talk too much in the classroom, rarely giving the children a chance to express what they know about a subject or ask for help. Children can actually "turn off" after a while. If the children are asked to repeat something, they can't remember it. This becomes a real problem if the teacher asks the children to take a test following an extended period of instruction (in fact, sometimes instruction of any length).

Teachers should slow down when speaking to children with language difficulties. They should be precise in both what and how they explain an idea or give directions. In addition, teachers should try to give only one instruction at a time.

Consider the following list of instructions with which a teacher prepares a class for a dictated list of spelling words: "Please sit down. Take out your pencil and paper. Write your name on the right-hand side of the first line of the paper. Write the date on the second. Write the numbers one to ten in a list on the paper. Now, spell the word *judge*." A child in any grade would no doubt have trouble remembering all the steps of these instructions, and the dyslexic child would never be able to carry them out.

Teachers must avoid telling a child to do three or four things in one breath. A dyslexic child needs to hear one direction and be given enough time to execute it before he is ready to progress to steps two, three, and four. Directions should always be clear, precise, and succinct and spoken slowly, distinctly, and loudly. Make eye contact, if possible, and take time to let your directions settle in. Break directions down into distinct parts and wait until the children have completed one part before moving on to the next.

If you discover that your child's teacher talks too quickly or gives too many directions at once, you probably won't be able to change his or her teaching methods. However, you can be aware of the problem and can try to correct it at home by going over the material at a slower speed and by trying to reinforce what has been taught in school. When the teacher is unable to assist, you need to compensate.

Fortunately for the dyslexic child, parents, teachers, and the public in general are becoming more sensitive to the plight of disabled learners and are making an effort to meet these children's needs in and out of school. This chapter has shown you how to work as effectively as possible within the school structure. The next chapters will show you how to help your child more effectively with his homework.

Case Study

Mark, Age 11, Grade 4
Mother: Francine, Age 40
Father: Steve, Age 46
Sister: Sandra, Age 13
Brother: Billy, Age 1

Reason for Referral Hyperactive and easily distracted in class. Several years below grade level in reading, writing, and spelling.

Mother Mark weighed only five pounds, four ounces when he was born, and I worried about him the first few years, but he developed normally. He walked at about twelve months and began talking during the next four months.

From the beginning he was hyperactive. As a baby he never slept through the night. He usually woke up at two o'clock in the morning and stayed awake from then on. By the time he was a year old, he was constantly on the go. He kept me worn out running after him. I was a nervous wreck throughout the second year because Mark was always in to everything.

He has always been shy and reluctant to play with more than one child at a time. When Mark turned two, I had a party for him and invited eight neighborhood kids. He walked into the room, saw the kids, and ran into the kitchen screaming. He wouldn't come out until the kids went home.

In any group he is the quiet child over in the corner looking on. He is especially reluctant to talk to adults, even those he has known for some time.

Recently, I took Mark to the airport to pick up his aunt. When she got off the plane and threw her arms around him, he ran to me screaming. I was embarrassed, but that's the way he acts.

Mark seemed perfectly normal in kindergarten. He got along well with the other children. The teacher called him playful. He was especially good with his hands, colored well with crayons, and generally impressed his teacher. But once he got in first grade, all progress stopped. He couldn't recognize the letters of the alphabet or form words. The school recommended that he repeat first grade. We felt that the school couldn't help him with his problem, so we transferred him to a private school.

He still didn't learn to read or write, so we transferred him back to public school, for second grade, where he began to develop some reading-writing skills. However, he still remains in the lowest reading group.

His sister teases him a lot, but he holds his own and teases back. Recently, Sandra and some of her friends laughed at him because he was carrying his teddy bear. He still has his original bear and takes it to sleep with him every night. He came to me in tears, and I did the best I could to console him. When the girls left the house, he dropped water balloons on them out of the upstairs window. This type of thing goes on all the time at our house.

Our family has gotten used to Mark's peculiarities, but the teachers complain that he never sits still. Apparently, every time the teacher turns her back, he goes to the board, walks around the room, or goes to the pencil sharpener. The teacher became frantic and insisted we do something.

Our family physician prescribed Ritalin to calm Mark down. We agreed at the time, but his father feels that it didn't do any good. Mark still runs around the house a lot, screaming and yelling. However, he is a good boy, and his father and I are anxious to help him in every way possible.

Psychologist This is an open, friendly child, who was eager to do what I asked. However, he was quite defensive about his school performance. He wouldn't admit to having problems, and when I asked about repeating the first grade, he said it was "because of illness."

As I began to test him, he was at first very quiet and passive. He yawned repeatedly and showed very little interest. When I brought out the blocks, he lit up and gave me a broad smile. He apparently loves working with his hands and his scores on object design and block assembly were outstanding.

Yet he tests dull-normal in social comprehension and auditory recall. He had a verbal IQ of 85 but a performance IQ of 114 (above normal). After I worked with Mark for about sixty minutes, he became highly distracted and restless. I would say he has a maturation problem because he simply can't concentrate. That is, he hasn't yet matured to the point where he can focus for long periods of time. I feel he may grow out of this problem. I also feel that Mark is an intelligent child, and that after therapy, his IQ should retest at a much higher level.

Evaluating Teacher Mark arrived accompanied by both parents. They seemed eager to learn as much about Mark's learning problem as possible.

In kindergarten, Mark participated eagerly in all the class activities. In first grade, however, he just didn't seem to comprehend anything. He couldn't even recite the alphabet and had no idea what sounds the letters made. He found putting words together next to impossible. Mark's mother insists the teacher didn't understand how to handle his problem.

When the school asked Mark to repeat the first grade, his mother and father pulled him out of public school and enrolled him in a private school. He didn't do any better there.

His parents then transferred him back to public school for second grade. There his teacher gave him a great deal of extra help and he learned to read and write. Now in the fourth grade, he is in the lowest reading group and stumbles over every word. However, he has almost reached grade level in math.

We gave Mark a standard battery of tests. During the testing, he yawned repeatedly, fell silent when uncertain, and smiled anxiously whenever we gave him something different to do. In general, he seemed quite uninterested in what was going on. Even when he did well on a test, he didn't talk or ask questions.

Mark scored at first-grade level on word discrimination and spelling tests and reads at a level somewhere between first and third grade. He is unable to read samples from the intermediate silent reading test usually given fourth graders and even had difficulty with second-grade material. He also had considerable trouble reading out loud (oral reading). In one test, he read two pages and made fifteen errors when trying to identify common sight words. When writing, he keeps mixing up letters: *men* became *nem, farm* became *fram, neck* became *ncek,* and so forth.

When asked to connect words with concrete items, however, he did extremely well. He is also near grade level in math. We feel that he can profit from further therapy. He is intelligent enough that he should, with help, overcome most of his problems.

The Follow-up After the evaluation, Mark completed eight years of therapy at a school that specialized in remedial instruction. His reading, spelling, and writing skills improved steadily. He came to comprehend school assignments. He learned to speak in front of the class and to express his ideas and opinions. Currently, he no longer confuses letters. His performance is normal, and he performs at or above grade level. He is planning to go on to college and should do well.

5

A Monster Called Homework

> Nothing in life is to be feared. It is only to be understood.
>
> —*Marie Curie*

For dyslexic children, there are few greater monsters than homework. Why? For two reasons: First, these students have short-term memories, and second, they approach understanding in a random manner. If they don't get help, homework can remain an unsolvable puzzle.

I have found that the majority of children in my classes can handle homework without difficulty. If I told my students to write about what they did over the summer vacation, most could put together three or four sentences explaining that they went to the beach, or camping, or to their grandmother's house, or something similar.

But when a child doesn't turn anything in, I wonder whether I've found a dyslexic. In one case, the parents later told me that their son would sit at his desk and say things out loud about what he did that summer, but when he tried to put these same thoughts on paper, he couldn't. Not only couldn't he make sentences, he couldn't write real words.

A Child's-Eye View of Homework

From a dyslexic child's point of view, homework can be a devastating experience. For him, it's like working in a vacuum. He doesn't really know where or how to start, and when he tries, he's usually wrong. Imagine how frustrating this would feel for anyone: No matter what you do, it won't be right.

One second-grade boy was asked to write a short report on the class field trip to a nearby garden. The gardener, a neighbor of the school, explained how she grew lettuce, tomatoes, and carrots. She showed the children the seeds, explained how she prepared the soil, and let a few children plant seeds. Then she let the entire class pick some vegetables.

At home, this little boy just stared at the paper. When his mother asked him what he was supposed to do, he told her that he needed to write a report. "What does the teacher want you to include in the report?" his mother asked.

"Nobody knows," the boy said. "The teacher made us walk over there and walk back, and when I asked if I should put that in my report, she yelled at me."

His mother tried to explain that he should write about the kinds of vegetables the woman had in her garden and what the class did when they were there. This didn't make any sense at all to the boy. When his mother left the room, he was still shaking his head in puzzlement.

A dyslexic has an unpredictable thought pattern. It's difficult to know when and how he arrives at a conclusion. He may begin to remember facts or figures in fragments rather than sequential order. Nevertheless, his thinking pattern is workable for him.

Another child's homework assignment involved looking up in the dictionary the meanings of three words the teacher had written on the board. First, he had to copy the words down—but he copied them backward. Of course, neither he nor his parents could find them in the dictionary. Finally, his parents had him call a classmate, who gave him the words, which they then wrote down for him. But when the child tried to look up the words, he couldn't. The dictionary words didn't make any sense to him, and the order of the definitions seemed mixed up. After about the fourth try, the boy dissolved into a crying fit.

As you can see, there is little purpose in having a child with dyslexia try to memorize ten or twenty words at home for a spelling test. He will miss most of them.

Unfortunately, in an educational system claiming to respect individual differences in learning, teaching methods often favor only those students who are able to learn logically. To really help a dyslexic, you should learn methods of adjusting his homework assignments to meet his particular manner of thinking.

Homework: The Link Between School and Home

Homework should be an important link between what is taught in the classroom and what is practiced in daily life. The key to learning something and using that knowledge is *connection*. Most dyslexic children cannot make this link on their own. If you help the child make connections, he will find homework or class work much easier. Academic subjects taught in isolation from the experience of daily life have no meaning for dyslexics; for this reason, some become bored with school.

One sixth grader, for instance, was assigned to read about a Civil War battle. After trying a few times, he gave up completely. When his mother asked why, he said, "It doesn't make any sense. They were riding horses and pulling cannons around with teams. That's not how I see wars fought on television. Where are the tanks, the helicopters, and the airplanes? That's the way to fight a war."

By the time children enter the middle elementary grades, their homework patterns are fairly ingrained. As subjects become more difficult to understand, students will need more time to solve problems, memorize facts, write compositions, and outline history. Unless children have established a sense of responsibility and discipline early, they will think of homework as a distasteful chore.

Set Up a Homework Routine

You are an essential link between the school and your dyslexic child. There are a number of things you can do to make homework less of a monster.

1. Establish a routine time for homework. This helps your child build a sense of responsibility and establishes homework as a daily habit.
2. Encourage your child at an early age to choose a special, quiet place to work: a favorite chair, a corner of the room, or a desk. Each night, have him look at a picture book for about ten minutes in his special place. Keep the time short at first and gradually increase it.
3. When your child can read, leave notes on the refrigerator or on a chalkboard in the kitchen. Keep the directions or message simple and succinct. Dyslexics have particular difficulty with messages that are too wordy or include more than one direction.
4. Build your child's self-esteem. Look for things he does well or remembers well and praise him for it. This should include verbal praise as well as a little surprise for special accomplishments. This will help the dyslexic overcome his sense that he can't do anything right.
5. Try to help your child break the homework assignment into steps so he can attack them one task at a

time. Homework will then become less threatening and distasteful.

The problem for most dyslexic children often begins when they try to remember the assignment. If your child has recurring problems remembering assignments, ask his teacher to send home written instructions. If your child is unable to read them, you can read them to him.

Homework, of course, does offer real benefits. At home, children are free to work and to think and to be creative, without the restrictions of the classroom. Homework also requires children to accept responsibility for their own learning.

BEFORE YOUR CHILD GOES TO SCHOOL

You should lay a foundation as early as possible that will later help to create a real link between your child's school assignments and his life, between abstracts and the concrete. Discuss everyday things with your young child: buying food, watching television, putting money in the bank, taking vacations.

Once the child is in school, he can link experiences and discussions to the pictures in his books and the words used to describe these pictures. This gives the child the ability to tell about his experiences and to link those experiences to action words that make sense for him.

I have seen this technique produce positive results. In one class, I had two dyslexic children. One little boy's parents hadn't taken the time to link what was happening in his daily life to words or to explain concretely the processes of living. The other child's parents took great pains to make him understand ordinary things. They explained why they worked, how they made money, why they put money in the bank, and how money was used to shop for groceries. His father even took him to his work for a couple of hours, let him deposit money in an account, and had him shop for groceries, making all the selections himself. For this family, a trip to the zoo became a chance to explain about animals and zoos and the need to save the animals. A boat ride became an opportunity to discuss and see how boats were made, what weather had to do with boating, and how boats are operated.

Both children had trouble reading, but the second boy was able to learn to read much faster, because he had made connections. He could also take part in discussions with much greater understanding than the other child.

As well as being related to life experience, homework is related to discipline, responsibility, and independence. You can begin to instill a sense of discipline by having your child make his bed, bring in the newspaper, or carry out the garbage.

One family insisted that the child clean his room in the morning and then sit in his favorite chair for ten minutes each day looking at a picture book. By the time he had to start doing homework, he had already developed a valuable habit. He was accustomed to spending time each day reading quietly, and he caught on to the requirements of homework much quicker than children who hadn't had this kind of training.

Helping with Homework

Homework has a specific function and purpose: It is designed to help the child remember, think about, and learn to use certain essential facts, processes, or strategies. Since the dyslexic child doesn't attack learning in a one-two-three fashion, you must give special care at home. Because a dyslexic child will ask *why* before *how,* you should start with concrete examples and then work backward to the principle on which the examples are based.

Help for Visual Learners

One child couldn't learn historical facts in the classroom, but he could draw pictures at home of historical events and tell his parents about them. This child's parents encouraged him to draw every day, and they set aside time to question him about the drawings. The results were a tremendous improvement in his history grade at test time. Even though he couldn't remember what the teacher said in the classroom, he could easily associate his answers about the pictures to the historical events. Below are other ways you can help your child with various subjects.

Help with Spelling

Another dyslexic boy was bright and enthusiastic but couldn't seem to spell the words I gave him on weekly tests. *Butterfly* would come out *butrefli* or *wave* would come out *wfa.* I was extremely concerned and asked for a conference with the parents. Together we worked out a home study system. At first, he would be given only five words a week, and the words would be the names of concrete things that he could see, such as *house* or *skyscraper.* His parents would review the words with him by showing him pictures of the objects. Then they would work on the patterns of sound-symbol relationships (*ay/oi, th/sh, ch* and *wh*). They would spell the word aloud to associate it with the object.

Within a short time, this child was spelling four out of five words correctly each week. Soon after, we were able to add abstract words. Over several years, this system was able to take the mystery out of spelling, and soon he could spell almost as well as the other children in the class.

1. Get a list of the sight words that your child's teacher uses, print them on pieces of paper, and place these words on the objects around the house that they designate.

2. Print the action words used by your child in everyday life, such as *walk, run, jump,* and *laugh.* Review these with him and have him act them out. Then dictate them to your child and have him write simple sentences using the action words.
3. Do the same thing for words with similar endings or beginnings and words that differ only by one vowel in the middle; for example: *an/ and, run/ ran, is/ as, come/ came, has/ have, live/ love.* These are problem words for the dyslexic child. (See the list in Appendix C for more problem words.)
4. Get a box of alphabet cards with lowercase letters. Each night during homework sessions, use them to spell problem words. If your child spells a word correctly, ask him to create a word that is similar to that word but has one vowel or consonant that is different. Limit the exercise to no more than five words a night. When all five words are on the table, ask him to pick a word and tell you how it sounds and what it means.

When the teacher introduces phonics, you can ask the child to find a letter that sounds like *ess* or *em* and relate the sound to its symbol. The sound-symbol relationship of letters is one of the most difficult problems for the dyslexic child.

You can also ask the teacher to require no homework for the child other than the exercises you do together. With consistent and regular one-to-one practice, your child will soon be able to recognize, recall, and use letters of the alphabet in reading, spelling, and writing.

Help with Reading

Try to begin reading assignments by asking your child a question about the material. In exploring the answer to it, he has a chance to put his thoughts in order. You might take advantage of this by reading the assignments to your child and asking him questions. This links the assignment to the experience in the book. Other parents put the reading assignment on tape so the child can listen to it during homework time.

Researchers find that past events are better understood by dyslexics when they are linked concretely to present events. Abraham Lincoln, for instance, was involved with a racial problem that affects Americans today. You could ask your child what Lincoln did to solve the problem and what is being done about it now. After you explore a topic like this with a child, you should help him put his thoughts in order to develop a theme. This takes time, but it is essential for the child's normal development and successful learning.

Help with Arithmetic

If your child is learning percentages, you can show him a newspaper advertisement that offers toys at a 20 percent discount and ask him to figure out the price of an item. By using a subject in which the child is interested and associates with enjoyment (toys), the arithmetic becomes more meaningful.

HOMEWORK AS PUNISHMENT

Homework should never be used as a punishment. One school instituted a policy of detention for children who misbehaved. They had to spend an extra hour after school one day during the week. While in detention the children either had to do their homework or write words they had misspelled at least twenty times. Both exercises are fine on their own, but when punishment is linked with schoolwork, children have a hard time separating the two.

Parent-Teacher Cooperation

It is important that you and your child's teacher cooperate. In most cases, the dyslexic child cannot do standard homework successfully. You should first set up a conference with the teacher to see what he or she can do to help. Perhaps the teacher would be willing to assign special exercises with which you can help the child at home. You can also see whether the teacher would allow your child to do no other homework except these exercises each night.

6

Helping the Dyslexic Child with Reading

Problems are opportunities in work clothes.

—*Henry J. Kaiser*

The previous chapters discussed various methods for teaching dyslexic children, all of which come under the head of the *auditory-visual-kinesthetic (AVK) approach.* Using AVK techniques, you can easily set up a program at home to teach your dyslexic child to read. Although the approach is similar to the one you use to help your child with homework, it requires color coding the alphabet cards and following a predetermined set of exercises included in this chapter.

You should start this program long before your child is assigned homework. Later, you can use these cards and exercises in homework practice.

Here is how to prepare the needed materials.

1. Cut fifty-one three-by-three-inch cards from heavy white paper (or use small index cards).

2. Print the lowercase letters of the alphabet according to the following color code, which will make it easier for your child to remember the letters and their sounds.

   Blue: With a wide, blue felt-tip pen, print the letters *b, l, m, n, s, v, z, w, d, j, g, y, r, th.* These letters are the voiced consonants. Pronounce them with the vocal cords and breath.

   Black: With a wide, black felt-tip pen, print the letters *p, s, c, k, q, x, f, t, h, th, ph, sh, ch, gh, wh.* These letters are the unvoiced consonants. Pronounce them with breath only.

   Red: With a wide, red felt-tip pen, print the letters *a, e, i, o, u, y.* Pronounce these letters with a short sound, as in c*at, it, not, cup,* and *net.*

   Orange: With a wide, orange felt-tip pen, print the letters *a, e, i, o, u, y.* Pronounce these letters with a long sound, as in *ate, eat, kite, note,* and *cute.*

   Green: With a wide, green felt-tip pen, print the letter combinations *er, ir, ur, or, ar.* Print the letter combinations *au, ou, aw, oo, oi,* and *ow.* These are special sounds.

   Also within the above divisions:

   Pronounce the following with the lips: *b, p, m, v, f, w, r, ph, gh, wh, er, ir, ar, or, ur.*

   Pronounce the following with the tip of the tongue: *n, z, s, c, t, d, j, l, th, sh, ch.*

   Pronounce the following with the throat: *k, q, x, g, h, y.*

Teaching Sight Words

Teachers introduce certain words by the *whole word method,* which means they teach them as sight words. These words represent a child's everyday experiences (see Appendix B for a list of sight words).

If you have not already made up the action word sequence, print the words on cards now: *run, jump, see, hear, sing, laugh, talk, walk, cry, eat, sleep.* When you introduce these words with the exercises, make learning them a game. For instance, show your child an action word and ask him to act it out.

For variation, take a card and slip it into the middle of the pack. Then flip through the cards. When your child recognizes the word, ask him to act it out, or demonstrate that he knows it by clapping. Later, you might dictate these words and have him write them down. Follow this by asking him to write a short sentence using a particular word. You might also make cards for articles in the house: *chair, table, dish, fork, knife, cup, pan, stove, window.* Follow this up by making short direction sentences, such as "Go to the window and look out," "Jump up and down," "Come and sit."

Set a Goal

Have your child tell you in his own words what he thinks his reading trouble is. Then, help him set learning goals. These goals depend on the child's age.

A six- or seven-year-old might want to learn the sounds of the letters to please the teacher, or he might want to learn to read faster to keep the other children from teasing.

The AVK-Cronin Sequence

Dyslexic children need a structured program that progresses step-by-step so they can associate what they hear with what they see. They then need to reinforce their learning by actually working with the letters and words. As already mentioned, this is called the AVK approach. My system employs this especially effective method for teaching dyslexic children to read and spell. Here is the AVK sequence I want you to follow:

1. Have your child listen carefully as you dictate an exercise (*auditory memory* training).
2. Have him take the letter(s) from the stack (or from your hand) and place them horizontally, from left to right across the table, directly in front of him.
3. Check the exercise for errors before moving on to the next step.
4. Have your child move the letter(s) into a vertical position (up and down) in front of him.
5. Have him write the letter(s), word(s), or sentence on a tablet or a sheet of paper.
6. Together, you and he should *check* the exercise for accuracy.
7. Have your child replace the cards in the stack before going on to the next exercise.

The above steps break the exercise into components that will lead your child to accurate and consistent *sound-symbol* relationships for reading and spelling. The horizontal positioning helps him with the proper *left-right sequencing of letters.* This is the most common spelling error a dyslexic child makes. The vertical positioning of letters checks for *auditory* memory.

Every child will be at various levels of accuracy. *Begin where your child is* and move on as soon as he establishes stable performance.

Do not think that your child has learned a word just because he has formed it several times. He must see it and use it many times and in different ways before it becomes automatic.

Take every opportunity to repeat the words and relate them to sounds. The more ways you can use a sound, the sooner your child will learn it. For example, if you are practicing the four phonic combinations of *h* (*ch, sh, th, wh*), take one of the combinations (such as *ch*) and ask your child to think of a word he knows that begins with that sound. He might think of words like *chair, cheat, chat, chum,* and many more. But in order to make this *ch* combination automatic, he needs to use it over and over.

The following exercises have been used successfully to help hundreds of dyslexics learn to read and spell. When you begin, ask your child to first name the letters of the alphabet. Explain that there are twenty-six letters. These can be combined to make hundreds of thousands of words.

Before starting the exercises, do a "scatter" check to find out whether your child recognizes the letters of the alphabet. Ask him to take out an *m* and put it on the table. If he recognizes the letter, tell him to put it back. Ask him to pick out a *g* and a *k*. Ask for several other letters. If he recognizes letters easily and correctly, move on to the next exercise.

Remember, as your child develops an auditory-visual-kinesthetic routine, he advances slowly but consistently toward independent, thoughtful, and correct study habits.

Exercise 1: Recognizing and Naming the Letters

Starting with the alphabet, ask your child to name the letters in order. Give him four or five letters at a time and take him through the AVK-Cronin sequence. Once he can name the letters, move to the next two or three, until he knows all twenty-six well.

Introduce one or two of the sight words with each session. Since the sight word cards convey something familiar in your child's life (*eat, sleep, sing, play, jump,* and so forth), he will connect the words with the actions and learn them quickly.

Learning the Letter Sounds

Every letter has a symbol (the letter itself, such as *a, b, c*) and a sound. The letters are divided into consonants, vowels, and sometimes combinations of either (*ae, ch*). I like to teach consonants first because I think they are easier for the children to remember and to sound out. I usually teach consonants by pointing them out in the words that children already recognize (like sight words). Use Exercise 1 to teach your child the general sounds of the letters.

Exercise 2: Alphabetizing

The child is now ready to put the letters in alphabetical order. Dictate the letters in the vertical columns; have your child find the appropriate letter cards and then have him put them in correct alphabetical order (see the horizontal columns).

Vertical	*Horizontal*	*Vertical*	*Horizontal*
a		r	
c		s	
d	a b c d	u	q r s t u
b		t	
		q	
e			
f		v	
g	e f g h	x	
h		y	v w x y z
		z	
i		w	
l			
k	i j k l		
j			
m			
p			
o	m n o p		
n			

EXERCISE 3: THE CONSONANTS

The consonants are:
b c d f g h j k l m n p q r s t v w x y z

Dictate the consonants listed in the vertical columns below. Have your child find the appropriate letter cards and then have him place them in front of him, horizontally (in any order).

Vertical	*Horizontal*
m	
p	m p r
r	
s	
t	t n s
n	
w	
v	b v w
b	
s	
c	s c d
d	
ch	
l	h l ch
h	
g	
q	g q u
u	
k	
l	j k l
j	
b	
l	
r	s l r b
s	

Vertical	*Horizontal*
g	
d	
t	d g t m
m	
v	
f	
t	f t x v
x	
z	
p	
l	p z j l
j	
x	
j	
z	y z j x
y	
ch	
l	
p	ch l p c j
c	
j	
th	
m	
j	th m g h j
g	
h	

Vertical	*Horizontal*	*Vertical*	*Horizontal*
r		t	
t		v	
s		k	
m	t s m n p r	l	k t v m l n
n		m	
p		n	
sh		f	
f		s	
w		j	
d	f sh d p n w	g	g j f s b t
p		t	
n		b	

EXERCISE 4: CONSONANT BLENDS

When your child has a good grasp of the consonant sounds and the short vowel sounds, introduce the consonant *blends.* Consonant blends are the sounds that two consonants make together, such as *dr* and *fr.*

Following the AVK-Cronin sequence, give your child the following words, which he must lay out on the table. Stress the sound of the consonant blend.

r	br	brag	brake	bride	brush		
	cr	cramp	crack	cream	crank		
	dr	dress	drink	dream	drop	drug	drift
	fr	from	frog	frill	froze	free	
	gr	grand	grab	grant	greed	grim	grade
	pr	press	print	pry			
	tr	true	train	trick	trap	trip	truck
l	bl	blue	black	bliss	blame	blank	
	cl	class	clean	clap	clip	clear	
	fl	flag	flop	fling	flare	flame	
	gl	glass	glory	gleam	glade	glad	

	pl	plot	plan	plum	plus	place	plane
	sl	slim	slam	slap	slip	slant	
s	sm	small	smash	smoke	smile	smart	
	sn	sneak	snare	snack	snort		
	sp	spell	spring	speak	space	spin	
	st	stay	stand	steep	stair	stem	
	sc	scan	scat	scalp	scare		
	sk	skin	skill	ski	skip		
	sq	squint	squash	squat	squad		
	sw	swing	swim	swell	sweep	sweet	

Teach these special consonant blends together:

ch	children	chat	chin	chill	chop	check	
wh	when	whip	white	while	whim	whisk	
th	thing	them	then	that	thank	thick	three
sh	shop	shed	shape	shade	shack		

th (voiced)		**th** (unvoiced)	
them	bathe	truth	thin
this	scathe	south	thunder
that	clothe	both	throat
those	breathe	north	three
these	mother	cloth	author
	father	mouth	method

ph (unvoiced)	**gh**	**wh** (unvoiced)
phonics	laugh	what
telephone	tough	who
graph	cough	when
	enough	where
		why
		which
		white
		while

Note: Be certain your child knows the meaning of the words he works with. If not, discuss a word's meaning so he can compose an oral sentence using the word.

EXERCISE 5: SPECIAL SOUNDS

The following sounds, called *special sounds,* are often difficult for the dyslexic child, since their pronunciation doesn't follow the rules he understands. Take him through the following exercises using the same sequence as for the other letters and sounds.

ow	how now down town crown brown towel
ow	slow crow glow flow yellow own show
ou	our sour sound found proud mouth shout
aw	saw crawl jaw draw dawn law yawn straw
au	cause caught because haul pause
oi	oil soil toil moist boil noise spoil
oy	boy toy royal joy annoy employ
oo	look cook took crook poor wood brook
oo	soon room moon stool cool tooth food

The Five r's

or	for horse fork north corn order
ar	hard part March farm car mar art
ir	first girl sir stir firm
er	her herd nerve perch
ur	church churn curb curt spurt

The Silent Letters

*w*r	wrote write wreck wring
gh	right light sight flight
g*h*	ghost
*c*k	back black clock luck neck
*l*k	walk stalk talk chalk
*l*f	half calf
*k*n	knew knee know knock knife knot

Caution: Do not divide special consonant combinations. For example, *pick/le,* not *pic/kle.*

Exercise 6: Short Vowel Sounds

The vowels are:

a e i o u (and sometimes) y

A syllable is a word or a part of a word pronounced with a single sound, such as *man* (one syllable) or *hu/man* (two syllables). A word has *as many syllables as it has vowel sounds.* (A vowel, such as *a,* can be a word because it has a vowel sound.) Before you teach syllable patterns, let your child *hear* syllables and perhaps clap or tap them out. Try tapping out *sit, a/rith/me/tic, sas/sy, from, kit/ten, chil/dren, pu/pil, can/dy.* (See Appendix D for rules about syllables.)

Announce the *name* of the vowel and have your child find it in the stack. Then ask him to lay it on the table. After he has done this a few times, ask him to work with the vowels in the list below following the AVK-Cronin sequence.

Dictate the following words and have your child make the words on the table:

a	can	ran	an
	at	bad	hand
	am	and	had
	man	has	fast
	as	tap	pan
e	men	red	get
	pen	send	left
	let	tell	sent
	best	help	went
	ten	yet	met
i	is	in	it
	tip	hit	him
	his	pit	big
	hill	left	dig
	win	did	pig

o	on	top	dog
	of	not	box
	doll	hot	hop
	mop	lot	stop
u	up	cup	but
	nut	run	just
	must	us	hut
	sun	bug	rut
	hug	cut	dust

Dictate sentences using words with the short vowel sound:

Words	*Sentences*
man a run can	A man can run.
cup is the hot	The cup is hot.
in sit sand the	Sit in the sand.
nap sun the in	Nap in the sun.

Make sure you tell your child that every sentence begins with a capital letter and ends with a period. Tell him that a sentence is a complete thought—it tells you something.

Exercise 7: Long Vowel Sounds

In every syllable, there must be *one* vowel sound. That vowel is short. But when there are two vowels together in a syllable or word, the first is *long* and the second is *silent.*

Dictate words from the lists below and have your child make the words on the table.

-ea-	-ee-	-oa-
eat	see	boat
seat	seed	goat
meat	meet	coat
read	week	toast
year	feet	boast
each	keep	
weak	tree	

-ie-	-ay-	-ai-
pie	say	rain
die	may	fail
tie	day	sail
	lay	nail
	pay	tail

a - e	i - e
ate	ice
came	five
wake	fire
gave	like
cave	ride
wave	

o - e	-y (i)	-y (e)
home	by	baby
hope	my	rusty
store	shy	bumpy
hole	fly	funny
	ply	lady

Exercise 8: Practicing Long Vowel Sounds

Dictate the words first and have your child lay them out. Then ask him to make a sentence using them. Again, tell him that every sentence begins with a capital letter and ends with a period. Continue to follow the AVK-Cronin sequence.

Words		*Sentences*
it a is	nice day	It is a nice day.
red coat got	the wet	The red coat got wet.
home the on	big is fire	The big home is on fire.
wake up men	ten the	Wake up the ten men.

Beyond Letter and Word Exercises

Once your child begins to recognize words and can sound them out, he needs to develop skills that allow him to read rapidly and retain the material. To develop these skills, he needs to acquire the ability to:

1. Read at different speeds.
2. Read orally with expression and meaning.
3. Develop vocabulary.
4. Comprehend factual material: recognize the main idea and the details that support the main idea; infer

meaning that is not in the material; recognize cause and effect and be able to summarize the material.

5. Read according to the purpose of the material: social studies, arithmetic, literature, poetry, history, English.
6. Read according to individual interests.
7. Read independently for fun and knowledge.

These skills can be taught every time a dyslexic child picks up a book. You must make him aware of what to look for in the reading material and ask questions before and after he reads.

You will not use every question and every technique listed here for every child. Pick what you think will work—tailor the material to your child's present ability and age.

First, tell him that the five *w*'s must always be kept in mind when reading anything—*what? when? where? who? why?*—and sometimes *how?*

Next, review the following suggestions and use those that seem appropriate, each time he reads. The suggestions include a preliminary discussion of the material, a discussion of what to look for when reading, and questions to ask after he has read the material.

Before Reading

Ask your child, Do you know or have you had any experience with the subject we are going to read? *What* is it about? *Where* did it happen?

While Reading

1. Ask your child to read each sentence and decide whether the sentence explains *when, where, why, how,* or *who?* You can give him practice by asking him to write the word that explains what the sentence tells.

Examples:

down the street	what when *where* who why how
out all night	what *when* where who why how
in a hurry	what when where who why *how*

2. Ask him to read for sequence or organization. Ask, What happened first? What happened next? What happened last?

   You may want to have him read the material first, then have him go back over some of it with these questions in mind. You can use this technique when reading stories to very little children: Who is in this story? What happened first? Next? Last? Why did you like this story?
3. Use chapter headings to form questions. Ask your child, Can you make a question out of the chapter heading? What was the most important thing that happened? How does the author hint at the main ideas?
4. Use picture clues. *What* important idea does the picture convey?
5. Ask vocabulary questions. *What* is the key word in this heading? *What* does this word mean in this sentence? *What* are some of the meanings of this word that you already know?

After Reading

1. Make sure your child understands the main ideas.
   What is (are) the idea(s) of this story? Event? Chapter?
   What is the topic sentence in this paragraph?
   What would be a good headline for this story?
2. Check to see whether your child understands the details.
   What facts show (ask about some details in the story)?
   When were they shown?
3. Check your child's understanding of the vocabulary.
   What new meaning did you learn for (pick out a word from the story)?

What does (pick a word) mean in this sentence?
What word could be substituted for (pick a word)?
What means the same as (pick a word)?
What word is the opposite of (pick a word)?
What is the key word in this sentence (pick a sentence)? In this paragraph (pick a paragraph)?
What word in this paragraph (pick a paragraph) creates pictures in your mind?

4. Check to see whether your child makes inferences.
   What does this mean to you (pick an idea in the story)?
   What do you think happened next (pick an event in the story)?
   How can you apply the ideas here to daily life?
   Why did the author write this story? This book?
   What kind of person was (pick one of the characters)?
5. Find out your child's level of appreciation.
   How does the author make you feel?
   What paragraph set the mood for this story?
   What kind of person was (pick a character)?
   How would you like to (pick something one of the characters did)?

Checking Progress

Each day as the homework session ends, you should ask your dyslexic child to tell you one thing he has learned. Ask him to tell you something he finds hard. This way, you teach him to take responsibility for his performance.

When you have material to grade, ask him to mark his work, right or wrong. You will be surprised how hard children can be on themselves. It is difficult to convince children who are so used to failure that they can do something right. When they are rewarded, it boosts their self-esteem.

The greatest reward I received during my teaching career occurred the day I worked with a group of sixth graders who knew very little about the use of adjectives. After several days of teaching adjectives, I passed out a paper to test the students' understanding. As I did so, I decided to work the test with them. On finishing, I announced that since we had done the paper together, I was certain they had followed along—so why not give themselves an A.

With great flourishes, they marked their papers with an A. As I said good-bye that day, the class rose up as one and clapped. That was nicest thing that happened to me in all the years I have taught and worth more to me than gold. What it said to me was that every child wants to learn when he knows how.

Encouraging Your Child to Read

To help your child enjoy reading, I suggest you take him to the library, get him a library card, and take out a book. Permit him to do his own browsing, since children will gravitate toward books they like and can read. Don't worry if he picks out a picture book (no matter what grade he's in). This will tell you how well he is doing.

When you get home from the library, leaf through the book and talk about the story with him.

1. Build an interest in a subject before your child reads about it. Do this by talking about firefighters and fire engines, airplanes, the police, and other subjects. If possible, take your child to the fire station, the zoo, the science hall, or anywhere that pertains to the reading material. Point out things he can later read about.
2. On your first trip to the library, talk about books and discuss how books are divided into chapters. Encourage him to read a chapter at a time. If he has trouble reading, you may want to read the first chapter, then take turns reading chapters.
3. If he needs to prepare an oral or written report, discuss the topic. Show him how to go to the library and pick out a book on the subject. Divide the book evenly by its chapters and decide how many chapters he should cover each day. Show him how to take notes and put those notes on

three-by-five-inch cards. Then put the card notes together under each chapter heading.

Building Spelling Skills

A child who spells a word must remember what the word looks like and remember the correct order of letters. If he writes the word, he must also organize his motor skills in order to put the word on paper.

Good spelling is the result of hearing the word accurately, associating the sounds to the letters in correct order, and writing the word.

When your child is a poor speller, is it because:

1. He doesn't know the alphabet?
2. He can't associate sounds with letters?
3. He hears the sounds in isolation and not in the order corresponding to the word?
4. He doesn't recognize the word when he sees it?
5. He can't (at the same time) hear the word, think how to spell it, and form the letters? To hear, think, and write is sometimes very difficult for a child who has a learning problem and is under time pressure.

A Method for Independent Spelling Study

Each child has to learn how to study a word. Spelling is both a multisensory and an intellectual process, involving the eyes, ears, hands, and reason. In spelling, your child should be taught to hear, see, say, and write as well as to understand the meaning of words. Here is a useful plan for helping him learn to spell:

1. Pronounce the word correctly and carefully. Never try to teach a word unless you know what it means.
2. Say the word in syllables.
3. Have him take the letters that make up the word from the stack and put them on the table *in syllables.*

4. If he makes a mistake, help him correct the mistake. Say the word again slowly so he can *hear* the mistake. Encourage him to do as much as possible for himself.
5. When he has the word correctly placed in syllables, ask him to push the word together to make it a *whole* word.
6. Say the word as a whole.
7. Talk about the meaning of the word.
8. Ask him to spell the word without looking at it, if possible.
9. When he can spell it without looking at it, have him put the letters back and then write the word.
10. Have him use the word orally in a sentence.
11. Last, have him write a sentence using the word.

Do this exercise as a part of your home teaching session. Do not use more than five words. Remember, if your child has ten words to learn because the teacher assigned that number, ask the teacher to reduce the number until spelling becomes only moderately difficult. It is important that your child learn to spell and use words correctly, both orally and in writing.

Spelling Hints

These hints are somewhat technical in nature and are best used in conjunction with spelling practice. Read them through, then refer to them as needed.

1. A one-syllable word must always have a vowel and that vowel is short.
2. In a two-vowel syllable, the first vowel is long and the second is silent.

   There will be exceptions to the above rules, but by the time your child becomes a fairly "good" speller, he will take the exceptions in stride. (English can be contradictory.)

3. When words begin with *qu,* the *u* is not considered the first vowel (*queen, quite, quiet, quack*).
4. In all *ue* words, the *e* is dropped before the vowel or consonant suffix: *due/ duly, argue/ argument, true/ truly.*
5. In any *dg* word, the *e* is dropped (as in *acknowledge/ acknowledgment, judge/ judgment*).
6. Watch out for *v.* It is always followed by a silent *e* regardless of the vowel before it: *love, glove, have.*
7. Words ending in *c* add a *k* before *ing*: *picnicking.*
8. Watch *oi* and *oy*: they have the same sound. Usually if you hear words with the sound of *oi* first, you spell it *oi* (as in *oil, ointment*). If you hear the sound of *oi* in the middle or at the end of the word, you spell it *oy* (as in *boy, employ*).
9. There are only two words that end with *yze* (with the exception of medical terms): *paralyze* and *analyze.*

The tools provided in this chapter have helped hundreds of dyslexic children and adults improve their reading and spelling and should help your child acquire the skills he needs for school success.

7

Self-Esteem and Social Skills

> Coming together is a beginning. Keeping together is progress. Working together is success.
>
> —*Anonymous*

All children need to be recognized in some way when they do something well, either with a hug, a gesture, or a word of praise that signals to the child that he or she is special. Recognition for something well done boosts children's egos. This helps them gain self-respect, confidence, and security.

Because of his failures, the dyslexic child rarely experiences feelings of self-esteem and self-respect. With each failure, his ego gets battered and beaten. I have seen dyslexic children who are subjected to constant failure shuffle along, head down and shoulders bent, in a helpless, hopeless attitude. This is the real tragedy of dyslexia.

The dyslexic child is prone to feeling dejected and angry, and he is usually withdrawn because he doesn't understand why he is different from others. He feels hurt and lonely.

He may also think that parents, teachers, and friends don't like him and pick on him all the time.

Sometimes these children have good reason to think this. I remember an eighth grader saying to his teacher, "When are you going to lay off me?" as she urged him to answer a question from his history text. The teacher did, in fact, badger him constantly; she sometimes even became sarcastic and scolded him in front of the class about not doing his homework.

This particular child, in truth, struggled over his homework every night. He simply had a difficult time reading the book and an even more difficult time comprehending its content.

Parents often feel helpless as they watch their dyslexic child move about seemingly without purpose. Although it is unrealistic to expect a child to succeed at every attempt, every child—dyslexic or not—needs love and appreciation. He may have problems, but you, as parents, must make your child feel that he is loved not for what he can or cannot do but for who he is.

Try to discover what your child likes to do and what he is good at and give him your encouragement and praise. Praise your child for every effort, large or small. Sometimes you might feel as though you're praising too much, but it is better to overdo it in order to help a child gain self-esteem. The dyslexic child needs your constant support and praise.

In my work at the Raskob Institute in Oakland, California, I often observed the dyslexic children who came into the learning center. They looked defeated and uninterested in learning. But after several sessions, I would notice a behavior change: They walked in purposefully, and seemed glad to be there. When this happened, I didn't really have to examine the child's academic skills to know he was making progress or to visit the classroom to see how he was doing. His attitude when walking, talking, and playing told me all I needed to know.

For instance, I had one child who refused to take off his cap; it was his security blanket. Neither I nor his other instructor ever demanded that he remove it. We sensed that once he began to feel comfortable with himself he would be comfortable with others and would be able to take his hat off.

One day, the Institute began a project of cutting steps into the hill that led to the back door. I put that boy in charge of deciding how many steps were needed and where they should be located and of choosing a team to help him dig the steps. When his team began to dig, the little boy went to work with great glee, throwing off his cap! I remember this incident well because I learned to watch for the subterfuges invented by children with learning difficulties to "hide" their problems.

Providing Early Training in Social Skills

In the life of every child, learning to communicate and to get along with other people accompanies the early development of language and sensory-motor skills. Although social skills are limited in childhood's early stages to smiles, coos, and gurgles, they are a crucial part of every child's basic educational development.

Parents should help their children develop these critical skills. All children can benefit from this type of training, but for the dyslexic child, it is especially important, because it gives him needed practice. Try to find one or two playmates for your child. Limit the number of playmates so that you can control the situation and keep your child from being overwhelmed. As time goes on, introduce him to other children, singly and in groups.

Be aware, however, that all children, but especially the dyslexic child, are distracted by too much noise or movement or by an unfamiliar setting. Overcome this by preparing your child in advance for social activities. For instance, if you intend to take him to a birthday party, tell him what to expect: children, noise, balloons, and presents. If you take him to church or shopping or visiting, explain what will occur and who he will meet. Talk it over when you get back home and answer any questions he may have.

The Dyslexic Child's Social Problems

Although all children need guidance in dealing with others, the dyslexic child must actually be *taught* how to get along with others. A dyslexic's social problems often occur because he misunderstands the situation or the actions of others. Sometimes dyslexic children overreact or respond incorrectly. Here are some examples of incorrect behavior.

Susan believed that everyone's toys belonged to her. Whenever Susan's mother took her to another child's house, Susan immediately grabbed the toys and refused to share them with anyone else. If another child tried to take a toy from her, Susan would scream at the top of her lungs, grab the toy, and start hitting everything in sight.

When Bill and Annie's parents had guests over for dinner, the children, aged nine and eleven respectively, made the situation embarrassing and uncomfortable. They interrupted constantly by making inappropriate remarks on irrelevant topics, and once they took the floor, they monopolized the conversation.

In school, Art, who was fourteen, always wrecked group projects because he didn't understand the rules: He couldn't wait his turn or he missed the point of the discussions. Art didn't intend to misbehave; in fact, he was eager and enthusiastic. But he tried too hard, and unfortunately, the results were always the same. Art's social awkwardness and clumsy behavior made his classmates dislike him. Later in life, these same tendencies cost him job after job and most of his friends.

Fortunately, most of these problems can be overcome if you provide some early training in what I feel are the three main problems children have when socializing.

1. Most small children are self-centered, though the majority grow out of this stage. Dyslexic children, however,

don't grow out of it. By the time they reach adolescence or adulthood, people find their self-centered behavior both irritating and odd.

2. Most children have difficulty learning to share. Dyslexic children have an especially difficult time, because they are developmentally several years younger than their chronological age. This means that a seven-year-old dyslexic often behaves like a self-centered two- or three-year-old child. As a result, dyslexic children are dependent on parents and teachers far longer than other children.

   Learning to share means learning to understand the feelings of others. At the preschool level, sharing means taking turns throwing or catching a ball or playing with toys.

3. All children crave attention, but dyslexic children have an exaggerated need. They either act out or provoke trouble to escape being ignored. This isn't abnormal behavior: It is simply delayed maturation. Don't punish them—help them.

You and your child's teachers should understand that the dyslexic child needs help overcoming these problems at every stage. If you can offer this help, your child has a chance of learning to communicate and get along with others normally.

Role Playing

Getting along with others is a complex art and is best taught by example. Children learn how to relate to others by observing their parents at home and their teachers at school. The dyslexic child learns all skills by concrete methods. As a result, role playing helps him interpret the facial expressions and body movements that indicate anger, sadness, irritation, happiness, pleasure, and confusion.

Some parents act out various books, such as *The Three Little Pigs,* when the children are small. This story is appropriate because it gives parent and child a chance to assume the roles of both pig and wolf. A child can be each of the three pigs and express fright and sadness; then he can be the wolf and show anger and aggression. The parent can show the child each emotion, complete with gestures and facial expressions.

You can also help your child learn proper behavior for upcoming events by role playing. When your child is invited to a party, for example, you and he can act out arriving at the party, giving the gift, and playing with the other children. Role playing is also helpful for the first day of kindergarten. Over and over again, act out what will happen on that day, well in advance of the actual event. After your child goes to school, see whether you and the teacher can set up a schedule for role playing, in the classroom or at home, to help your child overcome problem situations, such as playing with other children or working in a group.

When a child doesn't understand the results of his actions and persists with negative behavior, you can use a form of role playing to vividly illustrate the point. For example, join a group of children with your child and behave the way your child does. Grab and hold on to a ball, toy, or game. When the others object, ask them what's wrong. You—and your child—will be told that taking a toy is not good manners and is selfish. During this role playing, make sure your child has a chance to be the one who shares.

Positive and Negative

The dyslexic child will also have difficulty understanding simple, courteous behavior, such as smiling, looking a person in the eye, shaking hands, making pleasant comments, asking polite questions, or not interrupting a conversation. These behaviors can be discussed in terms of *positive* or *negative.*

Some parents use their video camera to illustrate this to the child. One mother videotaped her child in various social situations, such as two children playing together in the living room, four children playing with a wagon on the lawn, and many children throwing a ball back and forth. In these scenes, she captured her child grabbing a toy and running away, keeping the wagon for himself, and getting mad and hitting another child with the ball. She played these scenes a number of times, explaining why his behavior was wrong. Finally, she and her child acted out each of these scenes again, this time with the child behaving properly.

As your child grows up, you can apply this principle to more adult activities: baseball, basketball, the classroom, group activities, boy-girl relationships, and parties. Social skills become more important as the child shifts from dependence to independence and the influence of his peers becomes more important than that of his parents.

The Need for Acceptance

Probably more than anything else, children want to be accepted. But some go to extremes. Josh was desperately lonely—he wanted very much to be liked, to have a friend, and to be chosen as a member of a team. To attract attention, he often resorted to lying, stealing, bribing, or giving away his lunch. By the time he got to the fourth grade, he began running around with a rough crowd of older boys and then started dealing drugs.

Unfortunately, it is easy for a dyslexic child to become a social misfit because of his clumsiness and lack of social skills. He rarely has the social maturity to keep up with the pack. As a result, he often feels isolated, friendless, and inferior. One answer to this problem is to help the child develop a special talent. Let's look at this in more detail.

Developing a Special Talent

One of the best ways I know to help a child build confidence and self-acceptance is to discover and nurture his talents.

This is crucial for the dyslexic child. Parents and teachers should encourage a child to explore a number of interests and to develop them.

Encourage your child to try not only the familiar sports of basketball, baseball, and football, but many of the lesser known sports, such as ping pong, badminton, skiing, rowing, tennis, or archery. Participating in sports offers children satisfaction, companionship, and pleasure.

Encourage your child to try various arts and crafts, such as drawing, sculpture, pot making, and papier mâché, or enroll him in drama classes. If he is interested in raising animals or in gardening, suggest that he participate in community organizations, such as Boy Scouts or 4-H. Observe what your child does well and help him continue to do well in whatever way is practical.

Jay's parents worked with him for several years without noticing any improvement in his behavior. They did, however, notice that he was interested in the trumpet players he saw on television. When he became old enough to buy cassettes, he purchased those featuring such trumpet players as Al Hirt and Dizzy Gillespie. His parents rented a trumpet from a local music store and turned the boy loose for a couple of weeks. Shortly after that, they enrolled Jay in trumpet lessons. When the school formed a band, Jay was the first to sign up. During the coming months, Jay participated in a number of concerts put on by the school band and was praised by the band leader as one of the best trumpet players he had.

For the first time in Jay's school career, he was successful. His self-esteem soared, and although he never became a top student, his academic performance improved.

The development of special talents can help both dyslexic and nondyslexic children improve their overall performance. For dyslexic children, the development of unique and special talents opens doors that couldn't be opened any other way.

The Adolescent Dyslexic

In *No Easy Answers,* Sally Smith says: "Teenagers live by the rule of the pack. They band together against, or, at least, apart from the adult world." This behavior is as normal as that of the two-year-old who becomes difficult to handle because of his attempts to become an independent person. The same difficult process of seeking independence occurs for the adolescent, although this time, both parents and teachers are baffled. The child is now in no-man's-land, neither child nor adult. Many parents probably wonder if they will live through it, believing that if they do, nothing will ever be as difficult!

Some dyslexic teenagers do have the social know-how to fit into the activities of their peers. For others, their delayed maturation keeps them from acquiring the skills needed for independence. Physically, dyslexic teenagers grow taller, stronger, or prettier just as other teens do, but emotionally they still behave like much younger children. Too often, they become glued to the television set or simply idle their time away in senseless activities with undesirable companions.

Parents and teachers may say to a dyslexic, "Isn't it time for you to grow up? When will you stop acting like a baby? How long are you going to be like this?" The dyslexic teenager often responds with, "Everybody picks on me." It's hard to grow up feeling good about oneself under these conditions. And it's twice as difficult to convince a dyslexic that he can do anything well.

I remember Tom, whose mother told me he got an A in spelling. When I tried to make a big event of this success, he did his best to convince me that "the words were easy." But as a teacher, I knew better; teachers create tests using the week's more difficult words. When I told him that, he then insisted that the teacher liked him. This was a typical response. The dyslexic tends to picture his world as a series of mistakes and the gnawing feeling of his unworthiness may linger, despite his success.

It is important for parents and teachers to reinforce the idea that the dyslexic is intelligent and that he just needs more time to take a test.

Remember, dyslexic children especially need to be recognized when they succeed. Unfortunately, their self-esteem is intertwined with their learning problem. But as with other aspects of this difficulty, you can make a tremendous difference in your dyslexic child's feelings of success or failure. The way you treat your child makes all the difference in the world.

Case Study

Ben, Age 7, Grade 2
Mother: June, Age 38
Father: George, Age 43
Sister: Nancy, Age 10

Reason for Referral Functions at a low-first-grade level and refuses to attempt anything difficult. (Ben's mother died between the child's testing period and the referral.)

Father I love this little boy, but he has been a real problem since we adopted him when he was seven weeks old. Before he was a year old, he would scream every time we tried to put him down or left the room. The only choice we had was to let him cry.

As he got older, we couldn't do anything that displeased him without having him throw a fit. One time shopping with his mother, he pulled a box of cereal off the supermarket shelf. When she put it back, he started screaming and wouldn't stop. Finally, she had to leave her cart at the checkout counter and take him out kicking and yelling. The only thing that really works is to take him to the park and let him run.

Despite Ben's problems, he and June, his mother, became very close. She made it a point to spend a lot of time with him and to read to him for at least thirty minutes every night. She didn't get much attention herself as a child and vowed to make up for it with our children. Sometimes I thought she babied him too much. She died three weeks ago after a long illness and Ben is still in shock. I have tried to give him extra attention, but I will never fill her place in his life.

Our physician placed Ben on Ritalin about six months ago. This calmed him down some, but he fidgets and can't seem to sit still. I made a mistake and tried to take him to church last week. He squirmed in his seat, dropped the hymn book a dozen times, and finally wound up running down the main aisle. Naturally, they asked us to leave.

I'm afraid Ben doesn't get along well with other children. June used to ask other mothers to bring their children to our home to play. Ben, however, is very possessive. Every time another child would try to play with one of his toys, he would throw a fit. After a few times, the other mothers stopped bringing their children.

Ben had the same problem in preschool, kindergarten, and first grade. He is constantly fighting, and the minute another child displeases him, he starts to scream. Because of this, the kindergarten teacher insisted he was unmanageable.

We started him in public school, but because of the constant turmoil, and because he didn't seem to be learning, we transferred him to private school. He received a lot of attention and calmed down, but I can't see that he is doing any better academically. I just hope someone can eventually do something for him.

Psychologist Ben is a small child, who could be mistaken for a four-year-old. This may be part of his problem, because the other kids pick on him. The minute this happens, Ben starts screaming at the top of his lungs. The teachers put the blame entirely on Ben, but in my opinion, it's a symbiotic relationship between the teachers, Ben, and the other children. It's the teachers' responsibility to defuse the situation.

There seems to be a similar problem at home. Ben's older sister tries to boss him around and he defends himself by screaming. His mother was the unifying force in his life. She always gave him extra attention and tried to make things easier. He has been extremely withdrawn and depressed since her death and stays in his room most of the time.

I let him sit in the office for a while before I started working with him. I deliberately asked questions I knew he would have difficulty answering. He became fidgety and tried to avoid answering. When I persisted, he closed his eyes and started screaming. I calmed him down then and we started over.

I didn't learn very much from conventional test procedures, because every time something seemed difficult, Ben refused to go further. Surprisingly, some of his test scores, including his IQ test, were low-average.

I tend to believe much of his present learning problems are due to immaturity. He is highly distractible and unable to stay with a task. Because of this, I believe that if he is retested in a couple of years, we will discover that his IQ is slightly over 100 (just above average).

I believe that Ben will eventually be able to learn at grade level and highly recommend additional psychological counseling and remedial therapy.

Evaluating Teacher Although Ben is in the second grade, he is functioning at a low-first-grade level. In class, he is highly distractible and restless. He can't sit still for more than a few minutes. He doesn't seem to pay attention long enough to understand instructions. On most projects, he simply waits for the teacher to come along and do the projects for him.

Ben was difficult to test. He continually refused to do anything he expected to fail at. He refused to perform at times and attempted to control the examiner. In spite of this, we uncovered a number of problems.

He doesn't remember what he hears, often reverses letters and numbers, doesn't know right from left, and has a problem understanding what he hears. In our opinion, Ben needs therapy in a very supportive environment.

The Follow-up Ben entered therapy when he started the third grade and worked on the names and forms of letters, phonics, visual perception, printing, and similar skills. He progressed slowly, but after two years of remedial training, no longer fears failure and is able to read almost at grade level. His teachers report he has calmed down and is now quite cooperative.

8

The Adolescent Dyslexic

> Do not confine your children to your own learning for they are born in another time.
>
> —*Hebrew proverb*

For most children, adolescence is a time of turmoil, change, and growth. It marks the second most important period of development in the life of a human being. From the age of ten or eleven, a child struggles to grow up and become an independent person. He begins to see himself as different, unique. He struggles to be free and independent, yet still needs the security of being trusted, loved, and cared for.

The confusing thing for most adolescents is that the experiences of childhood no longer answer life's questions satisfactorily, so they turn away from the family for answers. Parents, of course, suffer along with their adolescent. Many throw up their hands and wail, "If we live through this, we'll live through anything!" When I left home, my mother felt terrible and cried. But she managed to joke: "I really haven't lost a daughter, and I have reclaimed a lot of hosiery." Remember that adolescence is a temporary state, and with your trust, love, and patience, your teenager will eventually discover who he is, where he is going, and how he will get there.

If you are confused and often frustrated by the antics of your teenager, know that he is confused and frustrated as well. Teenagers do care, and they do try, but because they operate in a no-man's-land where childhood experiences no longer explain life, they rebel in order to find their independence in a new, larger, and more complex society. They are no longer children and not yet adults, and they have no map to help them understand this unique journey. Remember, it is healthy to move on and become adult, independent, and responsible. Kahlil Gibran expresses it best in the following lines from *The Prophet*:

Your children are not your children
They are the sons and daughters of Life's
longing for itself.
They come through you but not from
you,
And though they are with you yet they
belong not to you.
You may give them your love but not
your thoughts,
For they have their own thoughts.
You may house their bodies but not
their souls,
For their souls dwell in the house of
tomorrow, which you cannot visit, not even
in your dreams.
You may strive to be like them, but seek
not to make them like you.
For life goes not backward nor tarries
with yesterday.

You are the bows from which your children
as living arrows are sent forth.
The archer sees the mark upon the path
of the infinite, and He bends you with His
might that His arrows may go swift and far.
Let your bending in the archer's hand
be for gladness;
For even as He loves the arrow that flies,
so He loves also the bow that is stable.

Despite the numerous and rapid changes in our society, bringing up children remains one of the most important tasks for parents. If teenagers can claim the love and trust of their parents, there is hope they will develop into the unique and capable adults they are meant to be. In this chapter, you will read about the four areas in which you can make a difference for your adolescent: self-image, organization, learning, and special talents.

Are Adolescents Different Today?

Adolescents today are not really very different from adolescents of yesteryear. Basic human nature remains essentially the same from generation to generation. It has always been difficult for the young to leave behind tested childhood experiences to become adults. Of course, the degree and impact of the struggle is more complicated now than ever before. Although adolescents are very much as adolescents have always been, nowadays they operate in a different world.

Louise Bates Ames of The Gesell Institute and her coauthors recently stated in their book *Your Ten To Fourteen Year Old*: "To believe young people today differ from their predecessors is a myth. Adolescents operate in a world in which the older generations are not certain of their own beliefs. They (adolescents) would be more sure of their values if the adults were more sure of theirs." Changing societal values have influenced adolescents most in such sensitive areas as sex, drinking, and the use of drugs. The problem for many is that they are getting mixed messages from adults. Adolescents have always bucked authority but the way they do it today differs from the past.

As one survey shows, in the 1950s, high school teachers listed chewing gum in class, skipping school, and disrupting the classroom as their worst problems. Today, those problems have been replaced by selling drugs, bringing guns to school, and extreme vandalism.

The Dyslexic Adolescent's Problems

If the dyslexic child has been guided through early childhood, and if his behavior has been carefully structured, he may not suffer any more than the normal stresses and strains common to all adolescents.

For most dyslexics, however, adolescence is an especially difficult time. Unready for adulthood, they become extremely confused. Despite their physical maturation, their emotions have not matured; they continue to struggle with unclear ideas and ideals and may still have no idea how to fit in with others.

Often, these children react in one of two ways. Some become hyperactive (because of an environmental overload of sights, sounds, and actions), and cannot focus on tasks. Others withdraw into themselves, spending most of their time daydreaming, at home and in school.

Jerome, for example, had trouble learning to read during the first few years of school. Listening to him wrestle with the words was so painful that the teacher finally stopped calling on him. On the playground, he was developmentally so far behind the other kids that they simply stopped playing with him or called him names. By the time he became an adolescent, he had withdrawn into himself. He always sat in the back of the room, never volunteered, and rarely talked to the other students; as a result, the other teenagers and the teacher almost forgot he was there.

Adolescents like Jerome are so quiet that they are often lost in the shuffle. Parents and teachers must be alert and attempt to identify these "lost" individuals. Both types of dyslexic adolescents, the hyperactive and the withdrawn, can be helped, as will be discussed later in this chapter.

Self-Image

Everyone needs to feel good about himself. One of the biggest problems for the dyslexic is that he may never have the opportunity to discover his strengths because his mistakes get in the way.

Marian, for example, struggled all through the primary grades to keep up with the other children and to please her family. In the sixth and seventh grades, the struggle became so difficult that Marian eventually began taking out her frustration on her teachers and her family. At school, she seldom talked to the other students but constantly disrupted the class. She refused to turn in her homework, even though she had struggled for hours to complete it. Sometimes, she sat and stared at the teacher when she should have been working. If she arrived at school early, she sat by herself on a step and read a book, ignoring anyone who said good morning.

At home, she refused to participate in family activities or chores. She constantly teased, taunted, or argued with her brothers and sisters and sometimes stormed into their rooms screaming. When her parents tried to intervene, she told them to stay out of her life. Although she needed help from her family, Marian alienated them.

When an adolescent behaves as Marian did, parents often experience confusion and frustration. Why is their son or daughter, who is verging on adulthood, acting like an incompetent child? This is difficult for parents who want to help.

Both parents and teachers must give dyslexic adolescents a sense that they are important, by affirming a positive perception of who they are and how they can make their lives happier. By working together, the home and the school can help a dyslexic adolescent change his poor self-perception from "I can't succeed," to "I can make it," "I will try," and "I can succeed."

Organization Skills

The dyslexic's difficulty with organizing and structuring his living space and learning skills has been mentioned before. The day-to-day strain of the numerous tasks requiring the dyslexic's attention, organization, planning, and remembering makes this child resist the reward of independence and self-sufficiency. You or your child's teachers need to introduce strategies for helping him cope with those tasks that demand organization and social interaction.

One of the best strategies is to encourage the dyslexic adolescent to make up checklists outlining each step of a particular task.

Small children often need to be taken step-by-step through elementary tasks. Often, dyslexic adolescents need the same help. You can't simply tell them to clean up their room. You must be specific, telling them to pick up the clothes and put them in the laundry or hang them up; pick up papers, putting away those that are needed and throwing the rest away; put items like radios and phones where they belong.

Some parents make up checklists and check off each item as it is completed. Have the dyslexic go over the list several times so that he can internalize the process and perform a task automatically.

Billy, for example, had to mow the front yard each Saturday during summer vacation. Unfortunately, he always missed spots, never emptied the grass bag, ran over the flower beds, and never put the lawn mower away. After complaining for weeks, Billy's mother made a simple checklist, which she put on a large chalkboard in the garage; the list took Billy through every step of mowing the lawn. He had to get the lawn mower, put on the grass catcher, start at the driveway and mow in straight strips to the neighbor's property on the other side, take off and empty the grass bag, and put the lawn mower back in the garage.

Every Saturday before he started, Billy's mother took him through the steps. At the end of each step, he was supposed to come back to the garage and check the next step. As time went on, the quality of the job improved.

This process of organization is important to the dyslexic and should be used for most tasks. These strategies can be applied to card games, chess, pool, and other games, so that organization becomes associated with fun.

Below are some additional strategies for daily survival that help the dyslexic adolescent learn organizational skills. Choose those you think will work for your child and use them as often as possible.

1. **Using transportation.** Teach your adolescent to use a map of the city and learn bus routes.
2. **Cooking.** Teach him to read and then follow a recipe. Teach him to make sandwiches, hamburgers, hot dogs; to heat soup, cook an egg, make toast . . . even boil water!
3. **Setting a table.** Teach him to set a place at the table correctly with knife, fork, spoon, napkin, plate, and glass.
4. **Making a bed.** Teach him to cover the bed with sheets, blankets, and an outer cover. Show him how to shake the pillows and place them on the bed.
5. **Shopping.** Show him how to check for necessary purchases, make a shopping list, estimate the amount of money needed, and make choices at the store.
6. **Eating at a restaurant.** Show him how to read the menu, understand the check, estimate the tip, and pay.

7. **Money.** Teach him how to count, make change, keep an account, and use a budget.
8. **Time.** Teach him how to read the clock and calendar and how to make a schedule for activities, dates, appointments, household chores, shopping, and school.
9. **Telephone.** Teach him the home telephone number and emergency numbers and how to dial numbers, answer the telephone politely, and ask pertinent questions.
10. **Reading.** Show him how a book or article is organized and how to find needed information.
11. **Filling out forms.** Teach him how to fill out work applications and other forms.

Remember, the dyslexic often needs much more time to complete tasks and also requires additional time between difficult tasks. Dyslexics suffer greatly from fatigue because they must concentrate fiercely in order to think in a linear mode, which is very difficult for them.

You need a great deal of patience to treat the adolescent dyslexic with understanding and affirmation. Both you and your child's teachers should not demand unrealistic goals. You should also not treat the dyslexic as a small child. The adolescent dyslexic needs to be supported every step of the way and yet still be encouraged to be as independent as possible.

Learning Skills

Hopefully, by the time the adolescent dyslexic reaches high school, his central nervous system has matured to the degree that many obvious dyslexic characteristics have smoothed out and become less noticeable. The "perpetual motion" that many dyslexics exhibit in early years has disappeared or diminished to a state more accurately described as "restlessness." His distractibility has subsided into daydreaming and his inattentiveness appears to be a lack of interest or poor motivation. This change is due to physiological maturation. That makes dyslexia subtler and harder to observe than in a younger student.

Dyslexia in an adolescent is also masked by the attitudes and disguises he has adopted along the way to escape the harsh criticisms of other students and teachers. Dyslexics will often mask their intense desire to learn and be like the other kids with a lack of concern. Joe, for example, a fourteen-year-old, arrived at the Institute and waited for someone to show him to a study room. As he waited in the hallway, he leaned against a doorjamb and muttered, "Gee, what a crummy place." This clearly wasn't true, because the Institute had just been built! However, Joe's remarks and attitude are typical of the behavior of a dyslexic adolescent trying to cover up his embarrassment, failure, or feeling of rejection.

Later, Joe refused to accompany his group on an outing to the grove adjacent to the Institute. He believed that the other kids would see him as a failure. Over the next six months, however, Joe began to acquire some of the missing foundation and social skills. By the end of the year, he had dropped most of his avoidance behaviors. I have found that most older dyslexics use subterfuge and, along with skill remediation, require some degree of professional counseling in order to remedy a poor self-image.

When working with the older dyslexic, it is natural for both teachers and parents to assume he has acquired foundation skills. But your adolescent will need to be tested to discover what level of instruction is necessary. You can purchase some tests from an educational supply store, or ask the school to administer them. Here are some of the learning problems that may remain and some of the things you can do to help correct them.

Spelling and Writing Problems

Dyslexics sometimes remain bizarre spellers all their lives. They may always transpose letters within words and add letters on to words, possibly because of poor auditory, visual, or phonic skills.

You can help the adolescent by having him review both the homework exercises in Chapter 5 and the reading exercises in Chapter 6. Take him through the remedial process until he becomes more proficient in both reading and spelling.

You should also have your child practice cursive writing. You can buy a book of handwriting exercises and have him practice writing on a regular basis. Practice gives a flow to letter formation and helps the dyslexic adolescent with spelling patterns as well. (See Appendix E for penmanship exercises.)

Short Attention Span

Dyslexics often have difficulty focusing on a particular task because they have a short attention span. A student who is forced to sit and listen regardless of how he feels will often tune out. This results in noticeable information gaps in some subjects. Students with a short attention span often find homework impossible to complete, and they are often slow and easily discouraged. They would rather say they don't know something than that they missed the information because they weren't paying attention.

For example, Linda could focus for only thirty to fifty seconds at a time. Unfortunately, if a teacher explained the same math problem for ten to fifteen minutes, Linda lost her after fifty seconds.

After thirty seconds, Linda would start drumming her fingers on the desk or begin looking out the window. Sometimes she would thumb through a book or get up and walk around the room. This infuriated the teacher, who would correct Linda in front of the class. Inevitably, Linda was sent to the principal's office, and Linda's mother would be called in. The dilemma was resolved when Linda was assigned to another teacher, who made sure all instructions were kept well within Linda's attention span.

Another possibility for a restless dyslexic is to require him to take several breaks while working on a task. Dave, who had trouble sitting through a discussion or a long stretch of class work, was given permission to leave the classroom and run around the building once or twice whenever he needed a break. By letting go for a few minutes, he was able to come back and focus on the task.

An older student is also likely to be handicapped by distraction from either internal or external circumstances.

Often, dyslexics are easily distracted and complain about too much noise, too many people, or too much going on around them. They are often distracted by the clutter of furniture, pictures, or wall hangings. You can help by removing all distractions and by keeping the room fairly quiet when they are trying to work.

Spatial Disorganization

Older dyslexics often continue to have poor spatial skills and cannot arrange material correctly. If told to arrange spelling words in columns, they often sprinkle words across the page. They scatter pieces of the same math problem on different parts of the page or can't center the title of an essay. These students keep messy notebooks and are disorganized when taking tests and doing homework.

Parents and teachers often label these students "careless." The truth is that they aren't careless: They simply have trouble with placement and organization. Julie, a helper in the school library, had a great deal of trouble putting books back in their proper place and checking the books in. Frequently, she would mix up the numbers, shelving travel books with biographies or medical books with cookbooks. She really wanted to do well on the job but couldn't organize the books or her motions.

The answer to problems like these, of course, is practice. Start with simple writing organization exercises, such as centering titles, and move on to more complicated problems.

Have the adolescent practice each of these skills until he achieves satisfactory standards.

Test Frustration

Taking a test is often extremely frustrating for the dyslexic. He may know the answer to a question and be able to answer orally but have a terrible time putting the answer on paper. Many adolescent dyslexics have failed so many times and for so long that they have little or no confidence in their ability to pass any kind of test. All their hang-ups seem to return when it is time to evaluate their progress in any one skill.

You can help in two ways. First, give simple practice tests so that the dyslexic can develop a test-taking habit. Try to keep these practice tests under fifteen minutes, otherwise your child may become restless and disinterested. Second, assure him that there is nothing wrong with making mistakes; everybody makes mistakes. It is what you learn from the mistake that counts. Mistakes offer opportunities to discover gaps in knowledge and to learn.

How can you help your adolescent learn from a mistake? Circle those answers that he gets wrong. Then go back to the book and read about the subject. You can ask additional questions about the material to help him see it from other angles. Most important, have him explain the answer; this helps him relax and avoid guessing. It also lets him improve while he competes only with himself. Self-competition gives a truer picture of what a dyslexic student is able to do.

Adolescents generally want to succeed, and they want to be liked by other adolescents and their teachers. It is important for you to help them retain their dignity in the face of mistakes and rebuffs and to let them know that you are behind them all the way.

Special Talents

Many dyslexic adolescents often exhibit outstanding talents; some are very gifted in music, art, mechanics, architecture, interior decorating, landscaping, science, painting, poetry, and even prose. In the past, I have had some outstanding dyslexic students who have done extremely well in these fields.

Mary Margaret was such a dyslexic. After graduating high school, she persisted until she was accepted at the San Francisco Conservatory of Music. There, she had the good fortune to meet a gifted musician and remarkable teacher who took an interest in her musical talent. After finishing the courses required at the conservatory, she enrolled in a local college, where she later received a bachelor of arts degree, with a B average in music.

Today, she strives to overcome the gaps in her academic education and in her social skills, while participating in concerts and singing regularly in a church choir. She also directs her husband's business affairs as she continues to triumph over dyslexia. Her life is interesting, busy, successful, and fulfilled, despite her constant daily struggle with fatigue. This fatigue is common to dyslexics, who spend every waking hour "on guard" in an attempt to structure their environment.

Art also found his niche in life by developing a special interest. Although he had trouble learning to read and was a terrible speller, Art got interested in cars at an early age. He often watched his father do minor repairs and tried to help. To promote this interest, his dad bought him his own set of tools and often let him remove some of the bolts or handle the simpler mechanical tasks. His father also bought him subscriptions to several car magazines. In high school, Art enrolled in a special mechanics class at the local junior college and learned to do a number of simple tasks. By the time he became a junior in high school, all his friends brought their cars to him for tune-ups or to be repaired.

"Sometimes," as his dad said, "the driveway looked like a parking lot."

On graduating, Art enrolled in an auto mechanics class at the junior college. When he finished, he went to work for a local garage, and three years later, he opened his own repair business.

While Art still had some trouble reading, he developed his special talents and was able to overcome many of his problems.

If you can't help your adolescent with a special interest, try to find a friend, relative, or neighbor who can help to direct your child's talent and provide needed resources. This attention can make a big difference in his life by providing a purpose, a social outlet, friendship, and support.

Supporting Your Dyslexic Adolescent

I have already described some of the things you can do to help your child develop self-esteem, become more organized, correct learning problems, and develop special talents. This, of course, is just the tip of the iceberg. As you go along, you should add to these anything that seems to work for your child. I want to suggest a few general rules.

1. Be warm and close to your children. As parents and teachers, we often think that we must always say something knowledgeable or teach something. Sometimes simply our presence, for support and comfort, is all that's needed.
2. Keep the door open for communication. Remember that someone once said, "Never let the sun go down on your anger."
3. Don't be afraid to set limits; adolescents want them. In addition, discuss your own values openly.
4. Remember that young people *do* want to learn and to lead useful, fulfilled, and happy lives.

5. Respect your teenager by treating him as an adult. Permit him to tell you what he thinks about drugs, alcohol, and sex. Talk with, not at, him. Try to be natural and honest and face any problem that may occur.
6. Know when to get help for yourself and your adolescent. No one can teach a child or adult who is extremely hyperactive, distracted, and unable to focus. In these extreme cases, I suggest consulting a physician. No parent wants to put a child on medication, but I have seen certain drugs, such as Ritalin and Dexedrine, calm hyperactive children so that they can control their behavior and improve their ability to concentrate. (See Chapter 3.) Medication is not for every child, but I have seen children on medication change miraculously: They listen quietly, attentively, and seem as if they have been reawakened to life. If a child needs medication, be sure it is monitored by a physician.

Adolescent dyslexics can be helped. They must, however, be allowed to retain their dignity in the face of mistakes and be convinced that, as they grow into adulthood, the sky is the limit.

Relationships and Adolescence

As well as acquiring useful learning and organization skills, it is important that a dyslexic possess basic human qualities. These are the qualities that make someone comfortable with himself and others comfortable with him. Dyslexics can develop these qualities by establishing close relationships with family and friends and learning to evaluate those traits desired for themselves and admired in others.

As Sally Smith says in her book *No Easy Answers*: "To be a good friend, to be a fine mate, to become a good parent are crucial goals for our society, and yet we do not educate our young people to fulfill them." Many people prepare for everything in their lives except relationships, yet relationships must be established every day—in the home, at school, on the job, in the community, in the country, and in the world.

The key to relating with others is how we see ourselves and how we see others in relation to ourselves. Dyslexics, who may grow up feeling unworthy, stupid, or lonely, have warped perceptions of themselves. Since developing relationships is the adolescent's most important task as he moves into the adult world, you must put more energy into helping him become a successful and contributing adult.

The dyslexic child, adolescent, and adult have difficulty establishing relationships because of their distorted interpretation of the feelings of others. They also have trouble reading facial expressions and communicating appropriately.

With the training and support described in this book, however, the dyslexic adolescent can find a comfortable place in his family, his school, and his world.

Case Study

Julie, Age 13, Grade 8
Mother: Roberta, Age 46
Father: Gerald, Age 44
No Brothers or Sisters

Reason for Referral Can't comprehend what she reads. Sometimes isn't in touch with the real world. Unsure of her own academic skills, she tries to avoid all school tasks.

Mother I'm convinced that dyslexia runs in families. Her father had some of the same problems that Julie has. He didn't learn to read well until he was in the last year of high school, and he absolutely hated school. Even today, he isn't a good reader and frequently mixes up letters and words. His father also had a similar problem. We just hoped Julie wouldn't have academic difficulties.

We noticed a problem about the time Julie turned three. She had absolutely no sense of right or left. Often, she would get confused walking home from next door. I had to watch her when she played with the neighborhood children to make sure she didn't get mixed up and wander off the wrong way.

A neighborhood mother once gave her a plate of cookies to take upstairs to the other children. She got sidetracked and wound up in the yard eating the cookies. This mother got so upset that she screamed at Julie, telling her she was stupid and would never learn anything. Julie came home in tears, completely upset. It took me an hour to calm her down.

To help her get ready for school, we used to sing the alphabet song, together, for hours. I also made big alphabet flash cards to practice with. In addition, I made sure that I read to her every night. She seemed to love this.

In our school, even the kindergarten students ride the bus. Most of the mothers drove their children to school for a few weeks. I wanted Julie to get used to the bus, so I rode it with her in the beginning. I also met her at her classroom after school, explained which bus to take, and let her ride to our bus stop by herself. When I thought she was ready, I let her come home alone.

Unfortunately, she got into a conversation with one of her friends and climbed on the wrong bus. They took her back to the school and called me. After that, I drove her every day and picked her up. She didn't ride the bus again until third grade.

Kindergarten was a disaster. Despite our practice, Julie had trouble learning letter names or sounds. She also couldn't cut along the lines or do many of the other assigned tasks. Her teacher apparently knew nothing about dyslexia and had absolutely no patience. One time when Julie couldn't identify one letter or the sounds, the teacher blew up and screamed at her. Julie came home that night almost in hysterics. I complained to the principal, but that didn't stop it.

Julie then became tense and unsure of herself. She decided she was dumb and started doing as little as possible to keep from failing. Because she stumbles over every word when the teacher calls on her, the other children tease her constantly. As a result, Julie has withdrawn into herself and dropped all her friends.

We try to help her, but now she wants to avoid anything she will fail at. Sometimes I think she's too concerned about failing, but then I'm not thirteen years old. I love my daughter and will do almost anything to help her.

Psychologist This is a very anxious little girl, who avoids failure by not putting herself to the test. She was extremely tense and uncomfortable when talking to me. She fumbled over her words when answering questions and avoided answering whenever possible. The Draw-a-Man test told us that this young lady was at least two years below her chronological age. She drew the man hesitantly, with few details, hands behind the back, no feet and no hair.

Julie is very unsure of herself. This was evident by her reluctance to even pick up her pencil and the apprehensive way in which she approached the drawing. She made very light lines, many of them unfinished. Then she would erase and start over. Several times, she erased everything and called that complete. Her strategy seemed to be to do as little as possible. This behavior is so deeply ingrained, that I suspect it started at an early age.

Julie also has some problems that might require medical attention. She seems tense and very uncomfortable. Her body movements are clumsy and jerky. She has difficulty breathing and seems to have a speech problem. In reading over her file, I would also conclude that Julie is socially immature. Her teachers indicate she doesn't have any friends and doesn't relate very well to the other students. Apparently, she refuses to talk at times.

Evaluating Teacher When Julie walked through the door, it was evident she was nervous and didn't really want to be here. Her records show that she has trouble with reading, writing, and spelling and has problems with mathematics. Julie was given a complete battery of tests, including the Peabody Picture Vocabulary Test, the Durrell-Sullivan Reading Achievement Test, the Wapman Auditory Discrimination test, and others.

She had a great deal of trouble reading and then answering questions. She would hesitate for some time on most questions, then give a short, halting answer that was often wrong. Frequently, we had to ask the questions several times before she would say anything. Sometimes she just refused to answer.

Her spelling is on a third-grade level. She seems to have trouble with visual and auditory memory and with associating short vowels. On the word discrimination level, she kept mixing up the letters *b, d, n,* and *u.*

The Follow-up Julie attended a remedial program for three years and responded well to a structured program that combined language, listening and speech skills, visual perception, silent reading, and vocabulary development. She improved steadily in both her scholastic and social skills and has achieved near grade level.

9

The Dyslexic Grows Up

> There are no barriers to our dreams so long as we believe in ourselves as the source of our happiness.
>
> —*Leo Buscaglia*

Richard was so expert at diagnosing and repairing cars that he soon earned the reputation of "the best auto mechanic in town." His business grew rapidly from the very beginning. Before long, he had to hire several assistant mechanics and a secretary, to handle the telephone and the files. Richard was a success. He was bright, articulate, and friendly, and he handled his employees well. But he had one problem. He was plagued by the fear that someone would discover that he could not read, spell, or deal with words.

As a teenager, Richard was labeled a "reading failure," rather than dyslexic. He participated in his school's well-meaning but inadequate "special education program." Fortunately, in his midthirties, encouraged by his business success and an understanding wife, Richard sought help for his dyslexia. Within a few months, he had studied sufficiently to acquire adequate reading, spelling, and writing skills.

Richard is not unique. There are many like him who are doing well in their chosen profession. But it is difficult to estimate the number of adult dyslexics in our society. Most experts believe that about 20 percent of the population has mild to severe dyslexia. Most of these people, studies show, are talented in one or more of the three-dimensional fields of mechanics, graphic arts and design, music, architecture, sports, or personal communication skills. But in two-dimensional, symbolic work, many are still functionally handicapped, struggling with reading, writing, spelling, handwriting, and sometimes, arithmetic (when it must be done by hand).

When freed from pencil-and-paper, school-type work, these people become highly imaginative, creative problem solvers who prefer "action" skills, where they use their hands. They have discovered, as Woody Allen says, that "there is life after school."

SURVIVAL SKILLS

The dyslexic adult continues to depend on the support and respect of spouses, family, teachers, and friends. With this support, and with an understanding of how he learns (often called *learning style*), the dyslexic can choose those strategies that are meaningful and helpful to his survival. I have included some of those strategies here. Essentially, these are concrete skills that trigger memories of school assignments, home chores, or duties on the job. There is some information on school tasks because adult dyslexics often take classes to improve the skills that were previously so difficult for them in school. Adult dyslexics also need to work these out for themselves without assistance.

All adult dyslexics need to be their own advocate. They need to explain their job difficulties, to realize that they have a right to those concessions that support them in their work, and to have ambition to lead productive and happy lives.

Helpful Hints for Adult Dyslexics

1. When taking classes to improve skills, use a tape recorder in class to record the lesson. Later, listen to the tape a number of times until you understand it completely. Then, write down the important points.
2. Use a tape recorder to leave messages at home or on the job site. This provides good practice for both communication and organization.
3. Put material needed for the next day's chores or jobs in an obvious place so you will see it when leaving the house. This is important because dyslexics often forget items that they can't see, and it may thwart short-term memory problems.
4. Carry a small notebook to jot down information needed on the job, for class work, for shopping, or for chores.
5. Put the car and house keys on a peg, where they will be easily seen.
6. Admit that you are dyslexic and request assistance that makes it possible for you to function at your full intellectual capacity. When attending a class, seminar, or speech, ask for permission to record it instead of taking notes. When taking a written driver's examination, ask to have someone read the questions to you.
7. You might ask for more time to take written tests. It is better to discover what someone actually knows than to never discover his capabilities. Although speed can be a factor in taking a test, knowledge and accuracy should come first.
8. Ask that your tests be given orally. Most dyslexics verbalize well, and outside of a stressful, written, timed situation, are excellent speakers.

Although there are many other strategies an adult dyslexic can use, these eight are the basics. I believe each adult dyslexic comes to know himself well and will eventually become ingenious at helping himself.

Learning Styles

Every dyslexic child or adult should be aware of his learning style. The older student or adult who knows how he learns can use his strengths and master his weaknesses. As already discussed, some dyslexics learn and remember best when they hear the material; others learn and remember best by seeing the material; others when the material is demonstrated concretely.

The dyslexic who learns best what he hears should be permitted to use a tape recorder for lectures, talks, and lessons, which can then be reviewed in spare moments at home, at work, or in the car. An employer might leave recorded messages or directions for the adult dyslexic worker.

The dyslexic who learns best when he sees a diagram, a picture, a graph, or a visual arithmetic problem should be permitted to use visuals to help with his presentations or explanations.

The dyslexic who knows how he learns and has command of his learning style also knows how to help himself most efficiently. This knowledge gives an adult dyslexic a feeling of self-worth and self-acceptance and gives him the sense that he knows what he's doing and how he can do or learn more.

When I first started to teach the primary grades, I knew that a stable sight-word vocabulary was important for reading. Therefore, when I was teaching poor or nonreaders, I would make an outline on the board of some images—for example, apples, pumpkins, footballs, or hearts—and put into these some basic words, either words that were confusing because of the similarity of their letters or words that must be seen many times before they can be remembered. They were easier for dyslexics to learn because of the "closure" formed by the images.

I never put more than six or seven words on the board because the game has to be played quickly and correctly. Some students would recognize a word immediately. They would then erase the word, use it in a simple, oral sentence, and pass the eraser on to another student. In the primary grades, I made this a daily routine, and the children loved it. Older students enjoyed it, also.

Early on, the only flaw in this daily game was me, the teacher. I thought that the children who recognized the words and their meanings quickly, on sight, were the bright ones. Although they *were* bright, they were not the only ones who were. I discovered that there were children who needed more than visual cues—they needed aural cues as well. These children were just as bright as the visual learners but they had a different learning style: They were auditory learners.

I learned a valuable lesson from these children. All of us can learn if we know *how* we learn!

Going Back to School

Eventually, many adult dyslexics go back to school to learn or relearn skills they had difficulty with as children. Adult dyslexics can be successful if they know their strengths and weaknesses. Below are a list of questions that will help adult dyslexics smooth out some of the problems that occurred in earlier schooling. Questions should be answered carefully.

1. What can I do well? Should I be studying art, auto mechanics, architecture, music, or something else? What college has strong departments in these fields?
2. What is difficult for me? Will the college I wish to attend accommodate my language weaknesses or will

they waive the requirement for me? (Talk to a counselor about this.)

3. Will I be permitted to use a tape recorder in class? If necessary, will I be permitted to take untimed, oral tests? (Talk to a counselor or to individual teachers or professors.)
4. Does the college I've chosen have counselors or departments that support dyslexics, especially during the first year?
5. Which school has the recreational activities and the extracurricular activities that I like?

Mentors and Special Talents

Many dyslexics are highly imaginative and creative problem solvers. Given appropriate support and training, they do well in life—they just have a different way of processing the information that they take in through their senses.

Margaret Rawson, a teacher of both children and other teachers, is a pioneer in the field of dyslexia. I have come to understand the wisdom expressed in her book *Dyslexics as Adults*: "The differences are personal, the diagnosis is clinical, the treatment is educational, the understanding is scientific." A talented dyslexic can grow into a competent adult who does well in a special area, provided that the area offers a worthwhile goal and personal satisfaction. As advocates, parents and teachers must be on the alert to identify a dyslexic's special talent or skill and make every effort to support a fulfilling and worthwhile interest.

Dyslexics should also seek out mentors who are eager to impart their knowledge and wisdom. Perhaps a boy with mechanical interest and skill will find a mentor to take him into his garage and, with patience and understanding, tutor him to success and personal fulfillment.

Many seniors also are eager to instruct or coach dyslexic children or adults. To contact the nearest senior center, check your local telephone book's yellow pages or check with an elementary or high school for suggestions on how you can help.

The Whole Person

The emphasis throughout this book has been on a holistic approach to the dyslexic's problems. I learned early in my career that both parents and teachers should do everything possible to develop the full range of a child's skills from birth on.

A dyslexic child who receives an early education in the concepts of space and time, organization, and social skills—and who has a curiosity about his world—is ready for school. He will be readier and more capable of learning to read, write, and spell in the early school years than a child who arrives in kindergarten or first grade without these skills. A child who receives support from his family and his school every step of the way often develops the desire and self-confidence to overcome learning handicaps.

The important thing to remember is that the dyslexic individual cannot overcome problems in a vacuum. His success requires that he continue to develop himself, from birth into adulthood to old age.

With family support and understanding, the dyslexic can learn to compensate for and, in a sense, overcome any and all handicaps. He can go on to become a happy, socially adjusted adult capable of contributing more than his share to society.

Case Study

Pat, Age 32, College Graduate
Husband: George, Age 36
No Children

Reason for Referral Difficulty with reading (no understanding or comprehension); deficient visual-motor skills accompanied by extreme directional problems.

Pat Music is my life. As a little girl I always heard tunes in my head. I learned to play the piano early, by ear. The music just seemed to be there. I couldn't, however, read music and even today I have trouble deciphering the notes. I have trained myself to do it, but sometimes it takes me a while to get them right. It can be painful. I'd rather just pick it up from listening. I can listen to most classical pieces once and then play them on the piano.

I love to spend hours in my music room. It's like being in a different world. I also enjoy passing on my love of music to others.

I can't tell you how difficult school was for me. It was a struggle at every level. When I finally graduated high school, I was determined to get a college degree. I failed college on my first attempt, since I couldn't read a textbook or understand the subject. Then I enrolled in the San Francisco Conservatory of Music and did much better, but it still took me six years to complete the program.

I have a visual problem that's been with me as long as I can remember. I have almost no visual coordination and it plagued me all the way through grade school, high school, college, and the conservatory. I have failed the visual test for a driver's license several times, even with glasses. Because of my visual difficulties, I have trouble keeping my balance when walking.

I can honestly say I have learned everything by listening. I just don't retain material visually. I have never passed a course by reading a textbook, taking notes, or taking a written test. At the conservatory, I took every class twice and did extremely well in those classes requiring only auditory skills. When I had to read or take a written test, I had problems.

After I graduated from the conservatory, I decided I wanted to teach music, so I enrolled in a teacher's program at San Francisco State. I did okay except for practice teaching. They sent me out to a local grade school. I tried, but

I'd hold up a paper to show the children how to make something, and I'd point to the wrong side. One of the children asked me to cut out a pattern and I couldn't do it.

When the children discovered I couldn't do some of the tasks any better than they could, they became unruly. Apparently, the skills needed to handle a class of first- or second-grade students are far different than those needed to teach music to one youngster at a time. The university finally asked me to stop teaching.

I would now like to obtain a master's degree and eventually teach music in a junior college. Those students are more interested in the music itself.

Psychologist Pat is an intense, excitable person. She rushed into my office twenty minutes late, all out of breath. It turned out that since she couldn't drive a car, she had taken public transportation from San Francisco to our location in Oakland, about twelve miles away. Apparently, she had missed a connecting bus.

Pat was neatly dressed, although she had a somewhat disheveled appearance. We first discussed her visual problems. As she talked, she became quite excited and intense about what a burden it had become. She couldn't, for instance, read a book and make a great deal of sense out of it. "I read the words," she told me, "but I never understand them. I have to pluck out the meaning piece by piece."

When I started asking questions, she kept trying to bring the subject back to her reading problem. When I asked about her years at the San Francisco Conservatory, she asked me if I didn't think her visual perception problems were responsible for her having to take every course twice. From then on, every time I asked a question, she brought it back to her problem. I just ignored this and concentrated on administrating the tests.

I discovered through testing that Pat possessed strong auditory skills. She answered every question rapidly, with a frantic air. Many of her answers were correct, but some almost seemed to answer a different question. Some of the answers were extremely superficial. She didn't appear to want to take the time to think the question through. One time, for instance, I asked her which subjects she liked best at the conservatory. Her answer was yes, and she wouldn't come back to the subject. She answered the arithmetic questions with the same flurry. As every student knows, arithmetic problems require some thought and precise answers. As a result, she didn't do very well.

When we turned to the performance test, she scored below average on everything. The object-assembly test was a good example of her problem. She was asked to put together a number of jigsaw puzzle pieces. She couldn't visualize the object she was working with and only got a few pieces together by turning them around and around until the edges would fit. During this entire procedure, she seemed quite agitated and talked continually. I just ignored her.

The Draw-a-Man test indicates an individual's psychological age and his or her psychosexual development. When I gave her this test, she drew the type of simple stick figure that you might expect of a five-year-old. It had only a head, arms and legs, and showed no differentiation between the sexes.

I was amazed to get this result from an adult. Pat confided that she had no concept of a man or a face. Her stick figure indicated an almost complete lack of visual memory and helps explain why she can't read. Pat obviously has superior intelligence but needs help with her visual skills.

Evaluating Teacher Before starting the silent reading test, Pat told me that she reads the words but they are a maze on the page.

I was extremely impressed by her. She has great visual handicaps, retains information with difficulty, and learns only by listening. Yet she completed six years of college on will power alone.

Her visual problems showed up continually on the tests. She did poorly when tested for sentence meaning. Her accuracy on the oral reading test was barely above ninth-grade level; she laughed continually while reading and kept making remarks about the material. She pronounced many of the short *a* sounds in words as long *a*. She also accented unexpected words in a sentence.

Her spelling scored on a ninth-grade level. She spelled seventy-three dictated words correctly, but she fragmented some words and arranged some letters incorrectly within the words. The visual screening was a disaster. She claims her optic nerves were destroyed by measles in childhood. We know she has been under a doctor's care for visual problems, but we have no idea how much damage has been done.

The Follow-up Pat attended therapy for reading skills with emphasis on organizational skills and visual word activities. She made substantial progress for three semesters. At that point, she discovered that she could go by public bus to a college in Marin, north of San Francisco. She then discontinued therapy and enrolled in the college. Later, she entered the music department, and several years later, earned an M.A. in music with a B average.

Glossary

Abstract Not concrete; not easily understood; theoretical.

Achievement test Measures an individual's knowledge of a particular subject, such as reading, spelling, mathematics. Scores are translated into percentiles or grade equivalents.

Alexia A brain disorder that causes the loss of the ability to read.

Aptitude test Taps an individual's ability or capacity for learning a particular task.

Attention deficit disorder (ADD) A disorder in which an individual is unable to pay attention. It varies in degree.

Attention deficit hyperactivity disorder (ADHD) The inability to control distractibility and select purposeful stimuli to focus on.

Auditory memory The ability to remember information processed through the ear.

Auditory perception The ability to distinguish sameness or difference in sound symbols, especially the short vowel sounds in words such as *bit, bat, bet, but, tot.*

Biological process A series of actions, changes, functions, or behaviors occurring in a living organism.

Central nervous system The brain and spinal cord; the system receives sensory messages and sends out motor messages. It controls the activity of the entire nervous system.

Chronological age (CA) Age in years and months.

Concrete learner Someone who learns through everyday experience or by seeing real objects.

Congenital Existing at birth but not hereditary.

Curriculum A list of courses or a program for a particular study.

Depression A syndrome of sadness, low energy, lack of motivation or interest, loss of emotional control, low productivity, and social withdrawal.

Development Stages of progression of growth in a trait or skill.

Dexedrine A stimulant drug often prescribed for hyperactive children.

Diagnostic prescriptive teaching A program that assesses a student's weaknesses and strengths as well as skills achieved, in order to work out a program of special instructional procedure.

Diagnostic tests In-depth measures of learning skills and styles.

Distractibility The impaired ability to block out stimuli such as noises, sights, and feelings.

Drug Any nonfood substance in abnormal concentration in the blood.

Dyslexia A dysfuntion of the part of the brain that processes linear information; the impaired ability to acquire proficiency in reading, writing, spelling, and math.

Expressive language The ability to express thoughts and feelings in correct speech patterns.

Fine-motor coordination Small-muscle activity, such as coloring within the lines, cutting patterns, and writing down letters or numbers.

Foundation skills Skills on which to build proficiency in reading, writing, and accuracy. Including sight word recognition, sensory-motor accuracy, and understanding of spatial relationships.

Grade equivalent The level of academic goals prescribed for each grade in elementary school and high school.

Gross motor coordination The ability to move the large muscles, as in jumping, running, throwing, or kicking a football.

Home schooling An alternative to public education, in which a child is taught at home by an adult.

Hyperactive Engaging in excessive movement, indicating distraction and restlessness due to overloading of the senses.

Hypoactive Underactive. May be caused by depression or fear of being wrong.

Individualized education program (IEP) A written plan for a special education student. Consists of goals and objectives for the child's instruction, including procedures for evaluating the program itself; devised by a team made up of school personnel, the parent, and the child.

Intelligence quotient (IQ) The number resulting from dividing a person's mental age as reported on a standardized test by his or her chronological age and multiplying by 100. Used to measure apparent relative intelligence.

Language A system of words used by a community of people with a shared history or culture.

Learning disability A particular difficulty a child may have in learning a particular subject according to the child's mental development level.

Learning style A behavior that characterizes an individual's approach to learning. An individual can remember best and therefore learn by what he sees, hears, or writes, or by a combination of these.

Least restrictive environment California Public Law 94-142 requires that students with learning problems be placed in a setting that meets their educational needs and closely matches the regular educational program offered their peers.

Mainstreaming The placement of an educationally disabled student in a regular classroom.

Maturation The completion of the biological process of growth.

Mental age A score obtained from an intelligence test that indicates a student's ability to learn, think, and absorb knowledge in relation to the average performance of other children of a given chronological age.

Motor performance The ability to perform coordinated movement of large or small muscles.

Nurturing The provision of love and care that helps a child to grow and develop.

Parenting The love, care, and guidance given a child by his parents.

Perception The ability to recognize, organize, process, and interpret stimuli received through the senses.

Phonics A code for connecting sounds to printed or written letters and their combinations.

Public Law 30-40 The education law signed by the governor of California in September 1990, which directed the superintendent of public instruction to develop program guidelines for specific learning disabilities, including dyslexia. (See Appendix F.)

Readiness Being ready to learn specific skills or tasks.

Reading-learning profile A graphic representation of a child's weaknesses and strengths consistent with that child's grade level.

Receptive language The ability to understand spoken language.

Relationship A term that indicates how persons relate to one another. People can be kind, loving, and considerate as well as unkind, unloving, and cruel to one another.

Remediation The process of correcting academic weakness by special instructional techniques or tutoring.

Ritalin A trade name for methylphenidate, a popular stimulant drug given hyperactive children. It appears to calm them and is not habit forming.

Sensory intelligence Intelligence or information gained through the senses.

Sensory-motor skills. The ability to coordinate perception with muscle movement, such as copying from the board, cutting a shape from paper, writing from dictation, or batting a baseball.

Sight words Words recognized instantly, without sounding out. Examples: *saw, was, said, and, come, go.*

Social Skills The ability to make judgments appropriate to a social setting or situation.

Special education An educational approach to meet the unique needs of handicapped children, which includes identifying the problem and determining the appropriate instruction; the program is administered by trained teachers and is monitored.

Special sound A sound made by a single letter in combination with one other letter such as *wh, ch, th,* and *sh.*

Support group A group of individuals with similar interests or problems who meet regularly and provide programs and services to assist one another.

Syllable A unit of language, consisting of a simple vowel sound alone or in combination with a consonant; words are made up of one or more syllables.

Syndrome A collection of symptoms or traits occurring together, characterizing a particular disorder.

Visual learner Someone who learns quickest and best by sight.

Visual perception The ability to interpret information taken in by the sense of sight.

Whole word method A method for teaching reading using whole words instead of phonics.

Bibliography

Many books have been written on dyslexia. I selected the readings listed here because they have been especially helpful to me as a teacher. However, this does not necessarily mean that I agree with or endorse all of the ideas contained therein.

Introduction

Smith, Sally L. *No Easy Answers: The Learning Disabled Child at Home and at School.* Cambridge, Mass.: Winthrup, 1979. Reprint, New York: Bantam, 1981.

Chapter 1

Brazelton, Berry T., M.D. *To Listen to the Child: Understanding the Normal Problems of Growing Up.* Reading, Mass.: Addison-Wesley, 1989.

Critchley, MacDonald, M.D. *The Dyslexic Child.* Springfield, Ill.: Charles C. Thomas, 1964.

Gesell, Arnold, M.D., Frances Ilg, M.D., and Louise Bates Ames, Ph.D. *The Child from Five to Ten.* New York: Harper and Row, 1977.

Hermann, Knud, M.D. *Reading Disability.* Copenhagen, Denmark: Munksgaard, 1959.

Huston, Anne Marshall. *Common Sense About Dyslexia.* New York: Madison Books, 1987.

Levinson, Harold, M.D. *Smart But Feeling Dumb.* New York: Warner Books, 1984.

Linkez, Arthur, M.D. *Writing, Reading, and Dyslexia.* New York: Grune and Stratton, 1973.

Lyman, Donald E. *Making Words Stand Still.* Boston: Houghton Mifflin, 1986.

Orton, Samuel. *Reading, Writing and Speech Problems in Children.* New York: Norton, 1937.

Pearse, Joseph Chilton. *The Magical Child.* Toronto: Bantam Books, 1980.

White, Burton L. *The First Three Years of Life.* Rev. ed., New York: Avon Books, 1991.

Chapter 2

Brainerd, Charles J. *Piaget's Theory of Intelligence.* Englewood Cliffs, N.J.: Prentice-Hall, 1979.

Breadley, Molly, and Elizabeth Hitchfield. *A Guide to Reading Piaget.* New York: Schocken Books, 1969.

Hampshire, Susan. *Susan's Story.* New York: St. Martin's Press, 1982.

Healy, Jane M. *Your Child's Growing Mind: A Guide to Learning and Brain Development from Birth to Adolescence.* New York: Doubleday, 1987.

Simpson, Eileen. *A Personal Account of Victory over Dyslexia.* Boston: Houghton Mifflin, 1979.

Chapter 3

Bradshaw, John. *The Family: A Revolutionary Way of Self-Discovery.* Deerfield Beach, Fla.: Health Communications, 1988.

Johnson, Marjorie. *Family: The Center of Formation.* Nashville, Tenn.: The Upper Room, 1991.

Smith, Sally L. *No Easy Answers: The Learning Disabled Child at Home and at School.* New York: Bantam Books, 1981.

Chapter 4

Annals of Dyslexia, Forty Years of Papers Reflecting the Best Research and Clinic Practice in the Field. Baltimore, Md.: Orton Dyslexia Society, 1988.

Chapter 6

Cronin, Eileen M., Ph.D. *Cronin Letter Box and Teacher's Manual.* Novato, Calif.: Academic Therapy Publications, 1971.

Cronin, Eileen M., Ph.D. *A Holistic Approach to Education.* Switzerland: University of Fribourg, 1968.

Gillingham, Anna, and Bessie Stillman. *Remedial Training for Children with Specific Disabilty in Reading, Spelling, and Penmanship.* 5th ed. Distributed by Anna Gillingham, 25 Parkview Ave., Bronxville 8, N.Y., 1956.

Vallet, Robert E. *Dyslexia: a Neuropsychological Approach to Educating Children with Severe Reading Disorders.* Belmont, Calif.: Pitman Learning, 1980.

Chapter 7

Glenn, Stephen H., and Jane Nelsen, Ed.D. *Raising Self-Reliant Children in a Self-Indulgent World.* Rocklin, Calif.: Prima Publishing and Communications, 1989.

Smith, Sally L. *No Easy Answers: The Learning Disabled Child at Home and at School.* New York: Bantam Books, 1981.

Chapter 8

Ames, Louise Bates, Ph.D., Frances L. Ilg, M.D., and Sidney M. Baker, M.D. *Your Ten to Fourteen Year Old.* New York: Delacorte Press, 1988.

Kline, Dris, and Stephen Pew, Ph.D. *For the Sake of the Children.* Rocklin, Calif.: Prima Publishing and Communications, 1992.

Nelsen, Jane, and Lynn Lott. *I'm on Your Side; Resolving Conflict with Your Teenage Son or Daughter.* Rocklin, Calif.: Prima Publishing and Communications, 1991.

Pearse, Joseph Chilton. *The Magical Child Matures.* New York: E. P. Dutton, 1985.

Smith, Sally L. *No Easy Answers: The Learning Disabled Child at Home and at School.* New York: Bantam Books, 1981.

Chapter 9

Maslow, Abraham. *Toward a Psychology of Being.* New York: Van Nostrand Reinhold, 1963.

Rawson, Margaret B. *Bulletin of the Orton Society.* Vol. 27. Baltimore, Md.: Orton Dyslexia Society, 1977.

Rawson, Margaret B. *Dyslexics as Adults.* Baltimore, Md.: Orton Dyslexia Society, 1952.

Appendix A

Before Your Child Starts School

Handling school tasks is not something that children pick up the day they walk into school. They have to learn how to learn, just as they must learn everything in life. They begin to learn from the moment they are born. Research shows that the inability to learn during the early school years is often due to lack of readiness.

When children enter school, their gross motor skills become refined, into sensory-motor skills—for reading, cutting, pasting, folding, and drawing; for writing, spelling, and math. The dyslexic child, however, does not develop a working sensory-motor connection during these early years.

It is impossible to accurately tell whether a very young child is dyslexic. Regardless, if you encourage your child to develop his physical, psychological, and intellectual skills to his full ability during his early years, you can expect him to have greater success in school than a child who isn't encouraged to develop these abilities. Here's what you can do to promote your child's development.

Period one. One to six weeks old: Coming to terms with life. At this age, your child needs physical comfort, love, and warmth to help him bond. There are two ways to help your baby.

1. Don't let him cry for long periods without attention. Offer him some response whenever you feel it is important.
2. Hold him in your arms while feeding. Smile, make eye contact, and murmur soothing sounds.

Period two. Six weeks to five months old: Connecting with the environment.

1. Continue to give your baby love and care. Pick him up frequently and respond to signs of distress.
2. Start developing specific skills. Place the baby on his stomach several times a day. This gives him a chance to raise his head and increase his visual-motor skills.

   Provide him with a mobile placed to the left of his head about twelve inches from his eyes. Keep these mobiles simple: For instance, two brightly colored cubes or two or three brightly colored cardboard circles. Commercial mobiles are too sophisticated.

   Make a human-face mobile using contrasting colors. This provides beginning practice for focusing and for using the eyes to *track,* an important skill for later reading.
3. Make up a bag of small objects of different sizes and colors that he can swat. Make sure that the objects are large enough that he cannot put them in his mouth.
4. Take him out of the crib or playpen whenever possible. Carry him into the kitchen while you cook. Take him into the backyard. Talk to him as if he could answer.
5. Keep your baby active. Inactivity slows the development of a baby's ability to learn.

Period three. Five months to two years old: The development of intelligence. During this period, movements coordinated with the eyes and ears become important tools for school.

1. Continue giving your child lots of affection. Touch him frequently, bending down and hugging whenever possible.
2. Provide the child with large objects, like pans, for banging. This is stimulating and helps him develop early muscle coordination.
3. Get him out in the world. Take him shopping and share the experience. Take him through the toy department and talk about some of the toys. This links words with objects through at least two of the senses.

   In the supermarket, let him put an orange or apple in your cart. Although he'll put it right in his mouth, he'll be learning something too. On the sidewalk, point out cars and the stray dog or cat. Some mothers take the child for frequent bike rides. This adds to his experience bank. Go to the park; point out trees and leaves, look at and smell the flowers.
4. Read to your child. Select large, colorful picture books. Point out pictures of a baby, a dog, a cat, or a duck and say the word. This links symbols to real life. The inability to make this link spontaneously is the basic problem that haunts the dyslexic child throughout his school experience.
5. Talk to your child frequently, even if you don't get much response. Smile and laugh. Respond to everything your child says.
6. Comfort your child if he makes a mistake or falls down. Explain that everybody makes mistakes and that every experience, pleasant or unpleasant, has its place. He learns from your reaction, your body movements, your facial expression, and your tone of voice. This is one of the most important lessons you can teach at this stage, because the fear of making a mistake cripples the capacity to think.
7. Help your child socialize. Encourage other parents to let their children play with him. Encourage other adults to talk to him.

Period four. Two to three years old: A taste for independence. This is an extraordinary growth period. It can also be a trying period for you as a parent. At about two years of age, the child attempts to establish a sense of independence and often shows an extreme negative attitude.

1. Continue to encourage your child to play with other children. Since small children often become overwhelmed by crowds, one or two people at a time are enough at this age.
2. Start giving your child directions now—don't wait until he starts school. Dyslexic children have trouble listening to directions, establishing priorities, and integrating them in an order of procedure. Give one clear direction for an activity. For example, "Go to the shelf." Later, you can add three, four, and five directions.
3. Teach the child choices and organization. Learning-disabled children frequently have trouble with both of these. Start simply. Ask the child to pick out and play with one toy at a time. This teaches choice, organization, and priority. When your child plays with a ball, insist that he put it back. Have him take the teddy bear off the bed, then put it back.
4. If your child has trouble with outside events, walk him through the expected scenario step-by-step.

   A learning-disabled child becomes overwhelmed by too many stimuli. He will never overcome this completely. Explain to him what is going to happen, then practice being at the party, the picnic, or whatever; take him through the actual event. Make a note of the mistakes, then anticipate and "train" for the next event.
5. Set up routines. Establish a definite bedtime, a specific time for breakfast, lunch, and dinner, a definite naptime, a time for play, and a time for reading. All schools establish routines that a child must adhere to. But if a child has not been introduced to daily routines until he goes to school, the results can be catastrophic.

6. Practice right and left, up and down. Dyslexic children nearly always have trouble with these four directions. Start correcting them now. Practice, and repeat, repeat, repeat. Once your child understands right, ask about the other hand. "What is that? Is it left? Everything on that side is on the left." Practice.
7. Listen to your child. Children must relate to others. When your child gets interrupted, it breaks the pattern and makes it more difficult for him to discuss his ideas the next time. A child who can't express his ideas won't be able to answer the teacher intelligently. Always remember, home is the first preparation for school.
8. Start teaching the concept of time. Keep it simple. It's enough at this age to teach now, later, today, yesterday, and tomorrow.

A parent needs to be patient. Some children walk, talk, read or do numbers before others of the same age. Parents fall into a trap if they think their child should develop skills in step with other children. The growth of learning skills is a progression from the concrete toward the abstract. That is what you want to instill and promote at this stage.

Period five. Three to six years old: Intellectual growth and interaction. Between the ages of three and six years, your child refines and improves the four main skills needed for school tasks: sensory-motor, language, curiosity, and social skills. Without developing these, no child is ready for school.

1. Encourage your child to take care of his room. Start with as few items as possible: a bed, a toy box, a chair, and maybe a chest of drawers. Help him pick up the things on the floor and make the bed. This helps develop an orderly way of doing things. Shift as much of the burden to your child as possible. This kind of training will help him later to keep his school desk neat and in order.
2. Keep reading. Use his favorite books. Relate the pictures to the story and let him use his hands and fingers to touch

them. Have him touch a word like *dog* and repeat it. Don't push or rush into reading. Let him develop at a natural pace. This again ties elementary motor skills to pictures, symbols, and abstract ideas.

Ask him to scribble a grocery list on a piece of paper. Later, you can show him a word on your list and relate it to the item you intend to purchase. Let him connect the thought, the scribbles, or the word to the item. When words are introduced later, even the dyslexic child will be closer to ready.

3. Encourage your child's interest in nature. Help him plant a small garden. Let him collect rocks, or encourage an interest in butterflies, birds, or even leaves. This helps him relate to and understand his surroundings—again, good preparation for school activities.

Many children need help in the early stages to be ready for school at age six. By assisting your child in every way possible during these early years, you as a parent can do a great deal to make sure he will be prepared to learn to his full ability by the time he starts kindergarten and first grade.

Susan, Age 8, Grade 2
Mother: Nancy, Age 37
Father: Don, Age 38
Sisters: Karen, Age 5; Nancy, Age 11
Brother: Jeff, Age 13

Reason for Referral "Slow" in all school subjects. Confuses lower with uppercase letters and makes many letter reversals within individual words.

Mother I feel sorry for Susan. Sometimes I think she is the family scapegoat. Her older brother and sister continually tease her. They hide her clothes and toys and tease her mercilessly.

Last week, I found Susan tied up in a closet, screaming at the top of her lungs. It seems that Nancy and Jeff convinced her to play Indians and Settlers with them. They said they had to tie up the Indian. Susan waited in the closet almost thirty minutes before she realized something was wrong.

I am tired of them making her the family scapegoat. I've scolded them, but when I'm not around they start up again. They also tell her she is dumb and can't do anything. No matter what they do, however, Susan comes back for more. She wants to please them so much that she'll put up with almost anything.

Sometimes her father and I feel that Susan isn't always in touch with reality. She doesn't have any idea what city or state she lives in. I believe this is just a matter of inattention. I admit I'm not very good at that either. When we moved here, I couldn't find my way around town originally, and as a young girl, I couldn't remember the name of my state or city.

Susan's problems, however, seem to run deeper than mine. She thinks that dogs have two feet and that cats are tailless, cars run by themselves without fuel, and that teachers live at school. Nothing I can say seems to change her mind. It scares me.

Susan loves people, especially adults. She wants to please so much that she'll try almost anything, but if the project becomes too difficult, she gets quite upset. I sent her into the kitchen to bring back a loaf of bread. When she couldn't find it, she started throwing things out of the cabinet.

Susan will talk an arm off if you let her. Whenever I have friends over, she talks from the time they arrive until the time they leave. She doesn't care if they answer her, she just likes to talk.

Susan loves music. She taught herself to play the piano at age three. When we saw how much she loved the piano, we gave her lessons. She blossomed quickly and was soon playing regularly at recitals. Now she plays better than some adults I know and is far better than her sister, who started lessons the same time Susan did.

Her father and I feel that the school is at least partly responsible for Susan's problems. They insisted on placing her in prekindergarten instead of regular kindergarten. As a result, when she started first grade, she was far behind the other children. She couldn't even recite the alphabet.

Now, they don't try to teach her to read and write. They just let her sit in class and won't call on her. The teachers won't admit this, but you can see the results. Susan had to struggle all the way through first grade.

I feel that if we can put her into a remedial program she will soon catch up with her classmates. The teachers keep telling me she has a developmental lag, but I don't believe it. You can't tell me that anyone who can learn to play the piano as quickly as Susan has can't learn to read if given the right help.

Psychologist I was pleasantly surprised when this attractive, blonde, chatty youngster walked into my office with her mother. She gave me a big smile and seemed genuinely happy to be here. Her mother, however, seemed tense and upset.

When I first started to work with Susan, we just talked. She seemed completely unaware of why she was here and told me her home was "very pretty" and that they had horses and a fire engine went by her house every morning. Her mother said they didn't have horses and that they seldom saw a fire engine in the neighborhood. Susan told me she liked playing with her brother and sisters but sometimes they were pretty mean to her. I gathered that they teased her and complained about her being in the way all the time. Susan, however, really wants to please them and will do almost anything if they will just play with her.

She fairly glowed when she explained how she jumped rope, then she got up and jumped all around my office. I had to bring her back to her chair.

When I asked about homework, her mood changed from one of elation to deep gloom, a scowl darkened her face, and she kept repeating "hard, hard, hard" . . . she seemed quite discouraged. I didn't push her any further.

Susan seemed to have trouble grasping concepts we use every day. I tried several on her, such as "stubborn as a mule" and "grumpy as a bear." She told me that she had seen a mule at a stable near her house and he seemed okay to her. And she laughed at the idea of a bear being grumpy. Then I asked her to fill in some words for me, such as "lemons are sour, but sugar is . . ." She just shook her head.

When I talked about some things she was unfamiliar with and asked her to remember them, she did quite well. Her auditory memory span was within normal range and so was her arithmetic score. Susan, however, is lacking in mechanical ability and comprehension. When I gave her some cutout figures and asked her to put them together, she tried for a few minutes, then gave up in disgust.

The Draw-a-Man test was also a disaster. She hesitated a long time before trying to draw the requested figure. When she did start, she fumed and fussed at every stage and erased a lot. The finished figure lacked hands and feet or any distinguishing characteristics. This clearly reveals a developmental lag in visual perception. Susan performed well when the tasks I asked her to do were routine, but she has almost no ability to solve abstract problems.

Susan really tried to please me. She cheerfully attempted everything I asked. But when I exceeded her ability, she quickly became discouraged. Every time I praised her, her face lit up. She has a wonderful attitude and should profit from remedial training.

Evaluating Teacher Susan's mother doesn't seem to have the slightest idea of what is meant by developmental lag. I have tried to explain this several times, but she blames the school for all of her daughter's reading problems because Susan was placed in a prekindergarten program instead of a regular kindergarten.

Her teachers have tried, but Susan has simply failed to read. Her reading and writing skills are those of a first grader and she reads so slowly that it is painful to listen to. In addition, she has no idea what she is reading. Recently, she read a simple story about a girl who grew up in Germany. When asked the girl's name and the country she grew up in, Susan couldn't answer. She also confuses lower and uppercase letters and makes many letter reversals, typical of a dyslexic child. It's sad to watch, because this little girl wants to please the teacher almost more than anything else.

However, she has a short attention span. We sent her to bring back three items and put them in order on a shelf. She was able to go to the closet and remember one item, a book, but coming back she wandered out the open door and returned only when one of the teachers went after her.

Susan shows mixed results from her academic tests. She tested above grade level for spelling and basic vocabulary but well below grade level for oral reading and general comprehension.

There is a silver lining to Susan's problems. Susan's strength is her desire to please and her willingness to keep working. Right now, she can't perform up to expectations, but we feel with her present attitude, and some remedial training, she can be expected to achieve grade level in most subjects.

The Follow-up Susan was enrolled in a program that stressed visual perception, word attack skills (phonics), and oral and silent reading. Since her strength was in her auditory memory, she was given oral tests only for the next two years. Despite her willingness to try, she improved slowly the first year. By the end of the second year, however, Susan could hold her own with other students at her grade level. Her friendliness made her popular, and her IQ retest scored well above average.

Appendix B

Basic Sight Vocabulary

a
about
after
all
again
am
an
always
and
any
are
around
as
ask
at
ate
away

did
do
does
done
don't
down
dear
draw
drink
I
eat
eight
every
is
fall
far
fast

help
here
him
his
hold
hot
how
hurt
on
in
if
in
into
or
it
its
jump

never
no
not
now
some
of
off
old
take
only
one
open
once
the
our
out
over

six
sleep
small
same
what
start
stop
step
white
thank
ten
that
tell
with
then
there
their

we
well
went
were
want
when
where
which
why
will
well
wish
who
white
work
would
write

be	fine	just	own	these
because	five	keep	pick	think
been	fly	kind	play	this
before	for	know	please	these
best	found	pretty	three	today
better	four	laugh	pull	big
from	let	put	to	black
full	light	together	blue	funny
ran	too	both	little	read
try	bring	gave	live	red
two	brown	get	long	right
but	give	look	round	under
by	go	run	up	going
make	say	us	call	good
many	saw	use	came	got
buy	goes	made	upon	man
say	can	very	green	may
carry	grow	me	seven	clean
men	shall	walk	cold	had
much	she	you	come	has
must	show	warm	could	have
my	sing	was	cut	he
myself	sit	wash	your	yellow

Appendix C

Problem Words

Poor readers do not have a stable sight vocabulary. They cannot recognize instantly and accurately words that look alike because of the arrangement of the letters. They miscall words and destroy the meaning of the sentence. Children need to practice these words often, in order to recognize them automatically, on sight. Lay out the individual problem words next to the words that are easily confused with them. Include these words in practice with the exercises in Chapter 6, just as you do with the sight words. Then ask your child to use these problem words in oral and written sentences.

am	and	are	big	pig
an	said	arm	dog	dig
there	on	cookies	here	run
three	no	children	tree	ran
back	blue	give	eat	has
black	true	gave	ate	had

get	have	pretty	little	in
gave	has	party	kitten	on
children	can	could	his	know
chicken	ran	would	her	knew
live	like	of	once	about
love	live	off	one	above
early	head	became	head	house
nearly	hand	because	heard	horse
home	new	men	fire	oh
house	now	man	fine	no
farm	knew	fast	it	went
from	know	first	if	want
work	but	saw	think	what
walk	put	was	thank	that
where	this	who	with	tie
here	that	how	white	die
pocket	then	very	went	wish
basket	them	every	when	wash
money	much	get	us	old
many	such	got	use	hole
how	wake	these	far	over
new	wall	those	fear	oven
some	first	round	soon	boat
come	fast	around	some	boot
desert	every	never	them	left
dessert	very	ever	they	lift
would	better	grass	dear	guess
could	butter	green	deer	guest

Appendix D

Syllable Rules and Word Structure

Syllable Rules

1. **Vowel-Consonant-Consonant-Vowel.** When a two-syllable word has two noncombined consonants at the syllable break—as in *kit/ten, bas/ket, par/ty*—the syllables break between the consonants.
2. **Vowel-Consonant-Vowel.** In a two-syllable word—such as *o/pen, ba/by, a/gain, e/ver*—the syllables usually break between the first vowel and the following consonant. But in words that consist of a combination of consonants (*ch, wh, sh, th*), the combinations go with the first syllable: *pock/et, wheth/er, kitch/en.*
3. **Words Ending with *-le*, Preceded by a Consonant.** These are usually two-syllable words, such as *ap/ple, sad/dle,* and *lit/tle,* broken so that at least one consonant goes with *-le.*

Have your child put the word together using the AVK-Cronin sequence explained in Chapter 6: First, have him place the syllables on the table individually, then have him push them together to form the word.

Word Structure

Words are structured by adding to the beginning or the end of a root word. Prefixes are added to the beginning of a word, as in ***up**hill, **down**hill, **re**read, **ful**fill, **re**think.* Suffixes such as *-s, -es, -ed,* and *-ing* are added to the ends of words, as in *nut**s**, glass**es**, dust**ed**, eat**ing**.*

Variations in Sound

These are difficult sounds for dyslexics.

c has a *soft* sound (*s*), as in *cent, city, cycle*

c has a *hard* sound (*k*), as in *can, cup, cat, cop*

g has a *soft* sound (*j*), as in *giant, gem, fudge, gypsy*

g has a *hard* sound (*g*-throat), as in *got, go, gas*

Appendix E

PENMANSHIP SKILLS

Whether using the left or right hand, your child should form letters correctly and legibly. Notice how he holds his pencil; he should hold it between his first finger and his thumb, with the pencil pointing up.

By the time your child reaches the third grade, he should be able to write his name, address, telephone number, the day of the week, and the name of the month. To evaluate your child's ability to write legibly, have him do this and observe the following:

1. Which hand does he use?
2. How does he hold the pencil?
3. Is the paper placed in a position for him to write comfortably?
4. Does he form letters properly?
5. Does he mix small letters with capitals when writing?
6. Does he reverse letters? Are there letters he cannot form?

Use your answers to these questions to find your child's writing problems and work on them regularly, as you do other exercises.

Since very young children often need help recognizing and forming letters, tell your child that he can make all letters from a circle and a straight line. Take the circle first. Have him begin at the top and move counterclockwise. He can make the following letters from a circle and/or a straight line: *a b c d e g o p s q*. From a straight line he can make: *f h i j k l m n r t u v w x y z*.

Appendix F

Parent Rights, State of California*

As the parent of a child who is being considered for assessment for special education, you have certain protections provided by the law. These protections include rights related to the assessment process and the development of the Individualized Education Program (IEP). In addition, you may appeal a placement decision if you disagree with the school district's decision, or you may file a complaint if you feel that the proper procedures have not been followed. Your rights are outlined as follows:

I. GENERAL RIGHTS

A. All handicapped children have the right to a free and appropriate public education (FAPE).

B. Individuals have the right to privacy and confidentiality of all education records, including the right to see, review, and, if necessary, challenge the records

*To learn whether your state has a similar policy, call your state office of education, special education department.

in accordance with the Family Education Rights and Privacy Act of 1974. (20 USC 1232(g))

C. Individuals have the right to request to be provided with a copy of the educational records prior to meetings and within five (5) days of the request.

D. All handicapped children, to the maximum extent appropriate, have the right to placement in the least restrictive learning environment, to the program with least restrictive alternatives, and the right to enjoy the same variety of programs as are available to the non-handicapped child.

II. RIGHTS RELATED TO NOTICE

A. All parents have the right to be fully informed in language easily understood by the general public and in the parent's primary language of all procedural safeguards and rights of appeal.

B. All parents have a right to a notice which includes:

1. A full explanation of procedural rights available to parents.
2. A description of the action the agency proposes to take.
3. An explanation of why the agency proposes to take the action.
4. A description of any options the agency considered.
5. The reasons why those options were rejected.
6. A description of each evaluation procedure, test, record, or report used as a basis for the action.

III. RIGHTS RELATED TO ASSESSMENT

Rights related to assessment include:

A. The right to initiate a written referral for assessment at the school district office after the resources of the regular education program have been considered and used.

B. The right to consent to an educational assessment by the District.

C. The right to have fifteen (15) days to give or withhold written consent for any proposed assessment(s), and to receive an assessment plan.

D. The right to initiate an independent assessment at public expense unless the public agency shows at an administrative hearing that its own assessment is appropriate. Procedures for obtaining such assessment shall be provided upon request.

E. The right to have an independent assessment considered by the public education agency with respect to the provision of an appropriate education to the child.

F. The right to present an independent assessment as evidence at any hearing regarding the child.

G. The right to an assessment that is designed to be free of racial or cultural discrimination.

H. The right to have a description of the procedures and tests to be used, and to be fully informed of the assessment results, including the right to a copy of the findings.

I. The right of students placed in the resource specialist program for more than one year to receive at least health and psychological screening at some time during the second year to determine if a further psychological assessment, health assessment, or both, are necessary.

J. The right to at least a three-year reassessment.

IV. RIGHTS RELATED TO INDIVIDUALIZED EDUCATION PROGRAM

Rights related to the Individualized Education Program (IEP) include:

A. The right to be notified prior to, and to participate in, and/or be represented at meeting(s).

B. The child's right to participate in the meeting(s) as appropriate.

C. The right to have the meeting within fifty (50) calendar days from date of receipt of signed consent to assessment, not counting days in July and August. An IEP shall be developed within thirty (30) days of the beginning of the next school year when a referral is made twenty (20) days or less before the end of the regular school year.

D. The right to have the meeting conducted in the primary language/communication mode of the family.

E. The right to be informed of available and appropriate program options.

F. The right to consent to the Individualized Education Program and to the placement.

G. The right to request an Individualized Education Program Team meeting.

H. The right to request a review and/or the development of a new Individualized Education Program.

I. The right to at least an annual review of the Individualized Education Program by the IEP Team.

J. The right to withdraw consent at any time after consultation with a member of the Individualized Education Program Team and after submitting written notification to an administrator.

V. RIGHTS RELATED TO NON-PUBLIC SCHOOL PLACEMENT

Senate Bill (SB) 769 rights include:

A. The right to appear before the local governing board and submit written or oral evidence regarding the need for non-public school placement for his/her child. Any recommendations of the board shall be considered at an Individualized Educational Program meeting to be held within five (5) calendar days of the board's review.

B. The right to have an Individualized Educational Program developed within sixty five (65) days of consent to assessment when a non-public, nonsectarian school placement is proposed and considered by the local governing board.

C. The right to a final determination of non-public placement costing more than twenty thousand dollars ($20,000), within ten (10) days of submission of the proposed placement to the State Superintendent of Public Instruction.

D. The right to another Individualized Educational Program meeting within five (5) days of receipt of the State Superintendent of Instruction's findings indicating availability of alternative placements.

VI. RIGHTS RELATED TO APPEALS

A. Circumstances:

1. The student, parent, or public education agency may request Due Process Hearing procedures when there is a proposal or refusal to initiate or change the identification, assessment, or educational placement of the child or the provision of a free, appropriate public education to the child.
2. The public education agency may request Due Process Hearing procedures if the parent refuses to consent to an assessment of the child to obtain a decision on the appropriateness of a program.

B. Due Process Hearing procedure rights include:

1. The right to meet informally with the school district's designee to discuss the issues.
2. The right to a mediation conference conducted by the State Superintendent of Public Instruction or his/her designee, or the right to waive the mediation conference.

   a. The right to have the mediation conference completed within fifteen (15) days of the receipt of written request, or to request a continuance.

   b. The right to be informed of the hearing date immediately following receipt of written request, and to have the hearing held at a time and place convenient to the parent and the pupil.
   c. The right to be informed of free or low-cost legal or other relevant services within three (3) days following receipt of written request.
   d. The right to examine and receive copies of any documents in the student's educational file within five (5) days after the parent makes the request orally or in writing.
   e. The right of the pupil to remain in the present placement pending all appeals.
   f. The right to be accompanied by one or more representatives.
   g. The right to examine the list of unresolved issues written by the mediator.

3. The right to an administrative hearing at the state level if the mediation conference fails to resolve the issues to the satisfaction of both parties.
   a. The right to a reasoned, written decision mailed within thirty (30) days following completion of the mediation conference or within forty-five (45) days following receipt of written request, if the mediation conference is waived.
   b. The right to have the hearing held at a time and place convenient to the parent and the pupil.
   c. The right to have the hearing conducted by an impartial hearing officer with knowledge of the laws governing special education and administrative hearings.

d. The right to be accompanied and advised by counsel and by individuals with knowledge of the problems of handicapped children.

e. The right to present evidence and written and oral arguments.

f. The right to question, cross-examine, and require the attendance of witnesses, including adverse witnesses.

g. The right to a written or electronic verbatim record of the hearing.

h. The right to written findings of fact and the decision.

i. The right to examine all evidence at least five (5) days before the hearing, and to prohibit any evidence not so disclosed.

k. The right to have witnesses excluded from the hearing, absent compelling circumstances to the contrary.

l. The right to have the hearing conducted without regard to the technical rules of evidence and those related to witnesses.

m. The right for non-English speaking parents to have an interpretor who is competent and acceptable to the party requiring a translator and the hearing officer. The decision and related materials will be in English, and where appropriate, also in the party's primary language.

n. The right to have the child present at the hearing and to have the hearing open to the public.

o. The right to appeal the decision to a court of competent jurisdiction.

4. The right to have an attorney paid for by the public education agency if the agency initiates the use of attorney services for actual presentation of written argument, oral argument, and/or evidence during a mediation conference or state hearing.
   a. The right to be notified, in writing, of the public education agency's use of attorney services at least three (3) days prior to the mediation conference, or at least ten (10) days prior to the state hearing, as appropriate.
   b. The right to be provided with a list of attorneys knowledgeable in mediation conferences and state hearings.
   c. The right to have the public education agency pay for the costs of the attorney services for which the parent is required to pay and for which the cost is not greater than that of the agency's own attorney services.
   d. The right to initiate, at the parent's own expense, the use of attorney services for actual presentation of written argument, oral argument, and/or evidence during a mediation conference or state hearing. When the parent initiates the use of attorney services, the parent must notify, in writing, the public education agency of the use of such services at least three (3) days prior to the mediation conference, or at least ten (10) days prior to the state hearing, as appropriate.
5. Parents or guardians may be entitled to have costs of attorneys' fees reimbursed if they prevail in court as a consequence of a due process hearing. The Handicapped Children's Protection Act of 1986, Public Law 99-732 states that a court may award reasonable attorneys' fees to parents/guardians of a handicapped pupil who is a pre-

vailing party in any action or proceeding brought under the procedural safeguards' section (section 1415) of P.L. 94-142.

VII. RIGHTS RELATED TO COMPLAINTS

A. Any individual, public agency, or organization may file a written complaint with the superintendent of a local public education agency or with the State Superintendent of Public Instruction alleging a violation of federal or state law or regulation governing special education or related services for an individual pupil.

B. Within five (5) days, the State Superintendent of Public Instruction shall determine whether the State or the local agency has jurisdiction over the complaint.

   1. If the State has jurisdiction, the State shall provide a written decision within thirty (30) days of the receipt of the complaint.
   2. If the local public education agency has jurisdiction, the superintendent of that shall:
      a. Investigate the complaint and report.
      b. Provide the complainant with a copy of the report.
      c. Schedule a hearing by the Board of Trustees.

C. The complainant may appeal the decision of the Board of Trustees within fifteen (15) days of the receipt of the Board's decision, or

D. The complainant may waive the right to a hearing before the local Board of Trustees and appeal directly to the State within fifteen (15) days after the receipt of the local superintendent's report.

E. Within thirty (30) days of the receipt of any complaint submitted on appeal, the State Superintendent of Public Instruction shall respond with a reasoned, written decision.

If you have any questions about your rights, please contact your district Office of Special Education.

Appendix G

Support Groups

Association for Children with Learning Disabilities
4156 Library Road
Pittsburgh, Pennsylvania 15234
1-412-344-0224

Center for Law and Education
955 Massachusetts Avenue
Cambridge, Massachusetts 02139
1-617-876-6611

Children's Hospital Study Center
University of Arkansas
Little Rock, Arkansas 72211
1-501-320-4666

Council for Exceptional Children
1920 Association Drive
Reston, Virginia 22091
1-703-620-3660

DCACD Learning Disabilities (Adults)
P.O. Box 9722
Friendship Station
Washington, D.C. 20013
1-202-244-5177

Developmental Disabilities Law Center
University of Maryland Law School
500 West Baltimore Street
Baltimore, Maryland 21201
1-410-706-3100

Launch Inc.
Department of Special Education
East Texas State University
Commerce, Texas 75428
1-903-886-5940

National Committee for Citizens in Education
900 Second Street, N.E., Suite 8
Washington, D.C. 20002
1-202-408-0447

National Youth Center for Law
114 Sansome Street
San Francisco, California 94110
1-415-543-3307

Ray Graham Association Institute for Human Development
340 West Butterfield
Elmhurst, Illinois 60216
1-708-530-4554

INDEX

To Order Books

Please send me the following items:

Quantity	Title	Unit Price	Total
______	______________________	$ ______	$ ______
______	______________________	$ ______	$ ______
______	______________________	$ ______	$ ______
______	______________________	$ ______	$ ______
______	______________________	$ ______	$ ______

Shipping and Handling depend on Subtotal.

Subtotal	Shipping/Handling
$0.00–$14.99	$3.00
$15.00–$29.99	$4.00
$30.00–$49.99	$6.00
$50.00–$99.99	$10.00
$100.00–$199.99	$13.50
$200.00+	Call for Quote

Foreign and all Priority Request orders: Call Order Entry department for price quote at 916/632-4400

This chart represents the total retail price of books only (before applicable discounts are taken).

Subtotal $ ______

Deduct 10% when ordering 3-5 books $ ______

7.25% Sales Tax (CA only) $ ______

8.25% Sales Tax (TN only) $ ______

5.0% Sales Tax (MD and IN only) $ ______

Shipping and Handling* $ ______

Total Order $ ______

By Telephone: With MC or Visa, call 800-632-8676, 916-632-4400. Mon-Fri, 8:30-4:30.
WWW {http://www.primapublishing.com}

Orders Placed Via Internet E-mail {sales@primapub.com}

By Mail: Just fill out the information below and send with your remittance to:

Prima Publishing
P.O. Box 1260BK
Rocklin, CA 95677

My name is ______________________

I live at ______________________

City ______________________ State ______ Zip ______

MC/Visa# ______________________ Exp. ______

Check/Money Order enclosed for $ ______ Payable to Prima Publishing

Daytime Telephone ______________________

Signature ______________________